PATHS, STEPS, & PATIOS
FOR THE GARDEN

PATHS, STEPS, & PATIOS
FOR THE GARDEN
Including 16 easy-to-build projects

ALAN & GILL BRIDGEWATER

NEW HOLLAND

First published in 2003 by New Holland Publishers (UK) Ltd
London • Cape Town • Sydney • Auckland

Garfield House, 86–88 Edgware Road, London W2 2EA, United Kingdom
www.newhollandpublishers.com

80 McKenzie Street, Cape Town, 8001, South Africa

Level 1, Unit 4, 14 Aquatic Drive, Frenchs Forest, NSW 2086, Australia

218 Lake Road, Northcote, Auckland, New Zealand

ISBN 1 84330 493 7

Editorial Direction: Rosemary Wilkinson
Project Editor: Clare Johnson
Production: Hazel Kirkman

Designed and created for New Holland by AG&G BOOKS
Designer: Glyn Bridgewater
Illustrator: Gill Bridgewater
Project design: Alan and Gill Bridgewater
Photography: AG&G Books and Ian Parsons
Editor: Fiona Corbridge
Project construction: Alan and Gill Bridgewater

Reproduction by Pica Digital PTE Ltd, Singapore
Printed and bound in Malaysia by Times Offset (M) Sdn. Bhd.

Contents

Introduction 6

Part 1: Techniques 8

Part 2: Projects 32

Introduction

When we were first married, we moved to an isolated, tumbledown cottage in the country. It was bliss—just the two of us…and two dogs, a cat, a couple of goats, two geese, and a hen. The garden was huge, with lots of apple trees and some derelict stone and brick outhouses. Though it was "romantic" struggling through the long, wet grass and mud to the well, and scrambling up the slope to the chicken house to retrieve eggs, we soon decided that we needed order. The first job was to pull down the outhouses and clear the bricks and stones. The next step was to build a brick path from the house to the well. Then we constructed a flight of steps up the bank to the chicken house.

Soon we were busy building projects for family and friends—a red brick path for Gill's parents, a flight of railroad tie steps for my brother, a vast decking patio for a family who lived by the river. Each project was an exciting new adventure. The starting point was to find out what our clients envisaged, and whether they had been inspired by something they had seen. We discussed the construction options, and whether old or new materials were preferred. Then we wandered around the site, exploring the possibilities and taking measurements, before establishing the final position for the project and working on the design. An added benefit of all these commissions was that we made friends with many local suppliers.

Building paths, steps, and patios in the garden is wonderful fun. If you enjoy working with bricks, stone, wood, mortar, and concrete, and are looking for a challenge, you are going to a get a great deal of pleasure from this book, and will learn some useful skills.

Best of luck.

Alan & Gill

HEALTH AND SAFETY

Many stone, brick, and woodworking procedures are potentially dangerous, so before starting work on the projects, check through the following list:

- Make sure that you are fit and strong enough for the task ahead. If you have doubts, ask your doctor for specific advice.
- When you are lifting large lumps of stone from ground level, minimize back strain by bending your knees, hugging the stone close to your body, and keeping the spine upright.
- If a slab of stone or balk of wood looks too heavy to lift on your own, find a better way of moving it—with a sack barrow, roller or pulley —or ask others to help.
- Wear gloves, a dust-mask, and goggles when you are handling cement and lime, cutting stone with a hammer and chisel, using the angle grinder, or sanding wood that has been treated with preservatives.
- Never operate a power tool such as an angle grinder, drill, or jigsaw, or attempt a difficult lifting or maneuvering task, if you are feeling tired or are under medication.
- Keep a first-aid kit and telephone within easy reach, in case of emergencies.

Part I: **Techniques**

Designing and planning

As with so many ventures in life, a successful garden feature is made up of one part inspiration, one part perspiration, and two parts organization. Be prepared to spend time thinking carefully about all the implications of a project, from taking measurements to considering how much help you are going to need—it will pay off. Arm yourself with a notebook and pencil, and start your advance planning campaign.

FIRST CONSIDERATIONS

- Do you live in an area with easy access to reliable suppliers and salvage companies?
- Will local companies deliver small quantities of stone and wood, or are you going to fetch the materials yourself—if so, will you need to hire a trailer or a truck?
- Is there adequate, safe access to your garden—a wide gateway, and room for trucks to turn?
- How are you going to move the delivered materials to the site? Are you going to do it yourself or ask friends to help?
- Is there a sawmill in the area, where you can buy a good range of rough-sawn and pre-treated wood?
- Do children and pets use your garden, and if so, is their presence going to affect your choice of project?
- Where are you going to do the woodwork? Are you going to work on a patio, in a yard, or on the lawn?
- Are any of your neighbors going to be concerned about the siting of a project, to the extent that you need to involve them at the planning stage? Consultation prevents conflict!
- Is your garden reasonably level and dry? Or is it swampy with soft, squashy lawns and stony outcrops? If so, what measures will you need to take to provide suitable areas to build on?

Choosing a suitable project

When you have decided what you want to build in general terms, you to need to focus on the details. You must consider all the aspects of your chosen project to determine whether it is suitable for the size and location of your garden and, of course, the size of your bank balance. You also need to assess whether you are strong enough for the work involved.

Let's say, for example, that you have chosen to build the Raised Decking (see page 114) with the Wooden Stairway (see page 120). Will you need to modify the size and shape of the decking to fit the available space? Is the decking going to look right in your garden? Is it suitable for your children? Will it upset your neighbors—for instance, will it overlook their garden? Are you going to have to move plants in readiness for building the decking? Or could you perhaps leave plants to grow through and around the finished decking? Does the number of steps in the stairway need to be adjusted to suit the slope of the ground?

Planning the project

Once you are clear about all the implications of building your chosen project, you need to plan out the logistics. When are you going to start building? Are you going to run it over several weekends, or are you going to start work during a longer vacation period? If you have put aside a specific weekend and are counting on the supplier to deliver the materials, are you sure that the supplier is able to oblige? Would it be better to order the materials to be delivered well in advance?

Do you require the help of some friends to complete the project, and if so, will you need to obtain additional tools for them to use? Don't forget that your helpers will probably also need feeding during the course of the day, so you need to buy provisions and sort out catering arrangements.

Will adverse weather cause difficulties? If you have to lay concrete, rain will hold you up unless you cover the area with a tarpaulin. Will it matter if you run a wheelbarrow repeatedly over your lawn? Heavy loads will inevitably damage the grass and create a muddy valley, so you may prefer to lay boards to avoid this. Will it be necessary to hire extra items such as another wheelbarrow or a concrete mixer? Are the children going to be a help or a hindrance? Maybe they should stay with friends for the day. Every detail needs to be planned out, from the minute the materials arrive to the moment when the project is ready to use.

Buying the right tools and materials

Though we have suggested using certain tools, you can of course make changes to suit your individual requirements. For example, instead of investing in a pair of portable workbenches, you could save money by using a couple of upturned tea chests. Much the same goes for the materials: if you would prefer to modify the project, such as by using salvaged bricks rather than new, or a different grade and size of wood, that is your choice. Most of the projects are flexible enough to accommodate such changes.

The quantities specified are generally very generous, especially for sand and cement. It is much better to finish up with a surplus than to run out of cement when you are halfway through laying a concrete slab and the shops are closed. When ordering materials, phone around for quotes, and ask if there are any bargains such as end-of-line items, or special offers. We always order well in advance, and pay on delivery. On no account part with money until the materials are on your property and you have checked them over for quality and quantity.

PATH, STEP, AND PATIO DESIGNS FOR THE GARDEN

Raised decking
A good feature for a bumpy, uneven site where you need to create a level area

Wooden stairway
A classic design for an outdoor stairway, which can be used against the Raised Decking

Rustic log ring path
A decorative path to complement a wooded setting

Railroad tie steps
A practical feature, which makes a very attractive addition to a rockery

Green wood walkway
The perfect way of bridging an area of boggy ground

Woodland steps
A small flight of low steps for an informal area of the garden

Decking tile patio
A dry, level area with many uses

Semicircular herb walk
A quick and easy way to build a path that incorporates a beautiful herb garden

Zigzag brick border path
This good-looking feature can be constructed to follow the shape of the flower borders

Classic stone sett patio
A useful feature for a small traditional garden

Natural patio
A charming addition to the lawn, providing an area of hard standing

Snake-pattern cobble path
A unique design that uses a combination of bricks, imitation stone setts, and cobbles

Elizabethan half-circle doorstep
A combination of brick and reconstituted stone set in a radiating pattern

"Crazy"-paved circular patio
An eye-catching, stand-alone feature

Art Deco steps
A stylish design made from wedge-shaped pavers

Decorative Victorian path
A path that is both functional and pretty

LEFT This garden plan demonstrates how the projects in this book might be used to fill your garden with attractive paths, steps, and patios.

Tools

While you can cut costs by using tools that are less than perfect—such as a saw that is not quite the right type, or a spade that is too short—a carefully considered tool will cut down on time and effort and make the task all the more enjoyable. A basic tool kit for the projects in this book is described below.

TOOLS FOR MEASURING AND MARKING

Level

Tape measure

Carpenter's pencil

Square

Bevel

Measuring and marking out the site

You need a flexible tape measure for setting out the site plan, wooden pegs for markers, string to delineate the shape of the foundation or footings, and chalk. A fiber glass tape measure is a good investment because it is waterproof and stands up well to the dirt and wear and tear involved in garden projects.

Woodworking tools for measuring and marking

We use four tools: a tape measure for establishing lengths and widths, a square for setting out right angles, a bevel for angles that are bigger or smaller than 90°, and a carpenter's pencil. If we need a long rule, we generally use a length of wood. A small steel rule is handy for marking out joints.

Leveling

You need a long-bodied level for checking the correctness of vertical and horizontal surfaces. If you intend to build a lot of projects, buy one made of wood and brass, otherwise get a cheap aluminum one. When working with uneven materials such as green wood or stone, the level is used as a guide only.

TOOLS FOR WORKING WITH WOOD

Claw hammer

Jigsaw

Crosscut saw

Electric drill

Drill bit for wood and metal

Flat bit

Cross-point screwdriver

Cordless drill/driver

8.4V

Mallet

Ax

Clamp

Sawing to size

Assuming that you have purchased all your wood ready-sawn to the desired width and thickness, all you need is a top-quality, hard-toothed, crosscut saw (designed to cut across the run of the grain). In fact, most modern saws can cope with cutting both across and down the grain. It is best to buy a new, razor-sharp saw for the project, and treat it as fairly disposable. At the end of a day's work, wipe the saw with mineral spirit and rub it down with oil.

Sawing curves

We use an electric jigsaw for cutting decorative curves. It is a very efficient tool, easily capable of cutting wood up to 12 in. thick. A variety of blades can be fitted to suit different types of wood. To use it, set the blade close to the cutting mark (with the bed of the tool resting flat on the wood), then switch on the power and slowly advance the tool to cut slightly to the waste side of the drawn line. When you have made the cut, switch it off and wait until the blade has come to a standstill, then lift the tool clear.

CAUTION

For tricky fixing situations where the workpiece is too big, heavy, or awkward to hold (such as a large decking frame), it is safer and easier to use a clamp to hold the components securely while you work.

Making joints

The projects generally use butt joints or over-lapping joints, with one piece of wood simply set close to another. But in one or two cases, end lap joints are required. To make these, you saw halfway through the thickness of the wood, and use the ax and mallet to chop out the waste wood along the run of the grain.

Screwing, nailing, and bolting

Screws, nails, or bolts are generally used for joining wood to make frames. An electric drill is required for making pilot holes for screws and bolts, and a vari-able-speed cordless drill fitted with a cross-point screwdriver bit for driving in screws. Occasionally, we use a hand screwdriver. In most cases, screwholes don't need to be countersunk: the wood is so soft that the screwhead will cut its own countersink. When it comes to nailing, we sometimes drill pilot holes, but mostly we simply drive the nail home with the claw hammer. When tightening up bolts, much will depend upon the design of your chosen bolts. We use one or other of our adjustable wrenches.

TOOLS FOR BRICKWORK AND STONEWORK

Mason's hammer

Bolster chisel

Angle grinder

Club hammer

Bricklayer's trowel

Pointing trowel

Cutting brick

Generally, it is best to avoid cutting bricks if possible. However, when the need arises, use a club hammer and bolster chisel for making precise cuts, and a mason's hammer for nibbling back a damaged edge. (A mason's hammer can also be used for removing mortar from salvaged bricks.) It is possible to use the edge of a bricklayer's trowel to chop a brick in half, but it is best to use a bolster chisel and hammer until you are more experienced. To cut a brick with a bolster chisel, set the brick on a block of wood, position the bolster chisel on the mark, and give the chisel a single, well-placed blow with the club hammer. Ideally, practice on a pile of old bricks before you start on those for your project.

Cutting stone

You need four tools for cutting stone: an angle grinder, a club hammer, a mason's hammer, and a bolster chisel. To make a precise cut—to break a slab of natural or reconstituted stone—start by repeatedly running the angle grinder disk along the drawn line (on both sides of the stone) until you have a groove. Then position the stone on a wooden block. Set the bolster chisel in the groove and give it a series of small taps until it breaks along the line. To trim a stone or to cut a jagged edge back to a straight line, set the stone on the ground with the edge to be worked on the far side, and use the chisel end of the mason's hammer to peck away the edge of the stone. Place the cut edge so that it is hidden from view.

Working with mortar

Working with mortar is great fun. We use a large bricklayer's trowel and a smaller pointing trowel. Once the mortar has been roughly mixed, it needs to be turned and mixed with the large trowel until it feels smooth like butter, and slices to show a firm, moist face. We use the large trowel for spreading mortar on the foundation in readiness for bedding bricks and stone, and the small trowel for buttering the ends of bricks with mortar and for pointing (see page 23). The large trowel is used with a scooping action (the mortar sitting on the back of the blade), while the small trowel is used with a spreading action, like a spatula.

When using mortar, the order of work is to spread it with the bricklayer's trowel, then bed the brick or stone in it, and finally slice off the excess mortar. As you work, use the level to test the levels of the bricks or stones. If the mortar is runny, it is too wet, so you need to add a small amount of cement to the mix; if it is too crumbly, you need to add a little water followed by a sprinkling of cement.

CAUTION

Cutting brick and stone is potentially very dangerous—eyes, lungs, hands, and feet are all susceptible. You must protect yourself by wearing a dust-mask, a pair of safety goggles, gloves, and stout work boots.

OTHER ESSENTIAL TOOLS

Gloves

Wheelbarrow

Spade

Shovel

Rake

Sledgehammer

Scissors

Snap-blade knife

Wire cutter

Wrench

Starting, fixing, and finishing

Where a project involves clearing a site, digging holes, mixing concrete, and generally moving earth, sand, and cement, a wheelbarrow is essential. A good wheelbarrow will not only save your back from a huge amount of stress and strain, but it will also let you move massive stones that are too heavy to lift. The best wheelbarrows have a large, inflated rubber tyre and a tip bar at the front, making it very easy to bounce your way over different levels in the garden, and just as easily come to a halt and tip out the load on the required spot.

A spade, shovel, garden rake, sledgehammer, and a good pair of leather gloves are also indispensible. Always choose tools that match your strength and height—trying to move earth and sand with a shovel that is too short, or banging in a post with a sledge-hammer that is too heavy, will cause you unnecessary stress and strain. If, when you are digging a hole or shoveling sand, you find that your hips or back ache, the chances are that the spade or shovel handle is too short. To help with large-scale projects that require earth to be moved, consider hiring in machinery—for example, a digger or earth-compacting machine.

Alongside the heavy tools, you will also need a pair of scissors for cutting plastic sheet, a pair of wire snips, a snap-blade knife, and a wrench. It is preferable to buy new tools and keep them to be used exclusively in the garden. This is because it is not a good idea to use scissors that may have come into contact with soil, possibly near drains, in the house—especially in the kitchen or nursery.

Materials

Building materials offer so much promise, excitement, and challenge! A disparate heap of materials – stone, sand, cement, wood, bricks—can be transformed, after a few days of great fun and endeavor, into a dynamic creation such as a path, patio, or flight of steps, which could enhance your garden for years to come.

WOOD AND WOODEN MATERIALS

3 in. x 3 in.　　*6 in. x ³/₄ in.*　　*2 in. x 1 ¹/₄ in.*　　*1 ¹/₄ in. x ³/₄ in.*　　*3 ¹/₂ in. x 1 ¹/₂ in.*　　*3 in. x ³/₄ in.*

Log roll border edging

Green wood post with bark　　*Skinned green wood post*　　*Specially grooved wood*　　*Dowel*　　*Ball*　　*Bark chippings*

Railroad tie　　*Wood stepping-stone*　　*Decking tile*

Sawn timber section

When you visit a sawmill, you will discover that there are a number of sawn timber sections available, such as 3 in. square-section posts, or boards 6 in. wide and 3/4 in. thick, all sold in lengths rangin.g from 6 ft. 6 in. through to 16 ft. 6 in. The wood is generally supplied in three ways: untreated and ready for painting, brush-treated with a brown preservative, and pressure-treated with a clear or greenish preservative.

Visit various suppliers to see what they have to offer, and to compare quality and price. Though a project might specify 6 ft. 6 in. lengths, you may be able to cut costs by buying 13 ft. lengths, or 40 in. lengths. Be flexible, and prepared to modify the design.

Green wood

Green wood is defined as freshly cut wood that is still wet or "green," as opposed to dry or seasoned wood. It can be purchased with or without bark, in its round, natural state, or as rough lumber. Traditionally, it is worked with tools such as the saw, ax, and drawknife. Green wood is ideally suited to garden projects for three good reasons. It is cheap, it instantly blends in and looks at home, and it is easy to work.

Decking and decking tiles

Decking can consist of anything from rough lumber straight from the sawmill, to fully seasoned surfaced wood that has been treated with preservative. In fact, decking can be just about any wood that you choose to use. Decking tiles, on the other hand, are specially designed for the purpose. Such tiles are usually between 12 in. and 20 in. square and can easily be made up from a number of identical thin sections that have been planed and pre-treated with preservative. All you do is arrange the sections to make a square duckboard or tile—seven on top and three on the underside— and fix them with nails or screws.

Bark chippings

Bark chippings consist of tree bark that has been ground up to a uniform size. It looks good spread on a path, or surrounding decking tiles, and when it eventually breaks down, you can spread it over the flowerbeds as a mulch.

Other useful materials

The projects use railroad ties, log roll border edging (half-round sections fixed to wire), slices cut from the trunk of a tree, and rough wooden balls sold as fence post finials. These materials can be purchased from fence-makers, sawmills, and garden centers. When buying railroad ties, try to search out some that are free from great blobs of grease and tar, and be ready to haggle over the price. We found huge differences in price between suppliers, with the most expensive from garden centers and the cheapest from companies specializing in salvage and demolition.

BUYING TIPS

- Ferret out the best prices. Phone around, ask for quotes, and then go to look at the products. Small shops are usually the most expensive, followed by garden centres, suppliers, and specialist dealers.
- Be flexible when it comes to sizes, and ready to change the shape and size of the project to suit available materials.
- Never buy anything unseen. Never let the delivery man unload without first checking the load. Always obtain a receipt.
- Try to buy in bulk whenever possible.
- If you can persuade one of your friends or neighbors to build a project too, you can both lower your costs by buying bulk orders of materials that you have in common.

WOOD FIXINGS

Countersunk crossheaded decking screw

Bright steel flatheaded nail

Galvanized fence staple

Zinc-plated, countersunk crossheaded woodscrew

Zinc-plated coach bolt, washer, and nut

Across the range of projects we have used countersunk, cross-headed decking screws; zinc-plated, countersunk cross-headed screws; steel nails; galvanized staples; and zinc-plated coach bolts with washers and nuts to fit. Wood fixings can be purchased in small packs, but it is much cheaper to buy them by weight (and it's always cheaper to buy them in bulk from a specialist dealer). You might only want a small quantity, but they aren't perishable, so why not buy more than you need and keep them for future use?

For interior woodwork we always use slot-headed screws (in situations where we are driving in a few of them by hand with a screwdriver), but when we are building garden structures that require lots of screws, we always opt for crossheaded screws used in conjunction with a cordless screwdriver. Crossheaded screws are designed to be driven in with a power screwdriver— they go in more readily than slot-headed screws and the process is easier than screwing in by hand.

BRICK AND STONE MATERIALS

Brick

Ceramic tile

Limestone block

York stone

Reconstituted stone square paver

Reconstituted stone
radius tile paver

Reconstituted stone paver
for circular patio

Reconstituted stone block for building walls

Rope-top edging in reconstituted stone

Ceramic border edging

Reconstituted stone
corner post

Patio section made from reconstituted stone setts

Cobbles

Yellow sand

Smooth gravel

Ornamental gravel

Bricks and tiles

Bricks and tiles are made from kiln-fired clay. The colors range from red-browns through to greeny blues, with all manner of subtle mixes and tints in between. Their textures vary from gritty and rough to glazed and shiny, and they look perfect in the garden.

Reconstituted stone

Reconstituted stone blocks and slabs are made from concrete with an aggregate containing the stone that they seek to imitate. Many reconstituted slabs look so convincing that they cannot easily be distinguished from the real thing. The stone comes in all sorts of shapes, sizes, colors, and textures—tessellating shapes that look like red quarry tiles, sandstone paving slabs, on-edge tiles, sandstone flagstones, ceramic rope-topped edging tiles, slabs made to look old and worn, and many other forms and designs. If you want to cut costs, reconstituted stone is a great idea.

Natural stone

The best types of stone to use in the garden are limestone, sandstone, and granite. Smooth, white limestone boulders are perfect as a feature edging. Sandstone, ranging in color from pinky-brown to blackish green, is a good choice for dry-stone walling, stepping-stones, and flagstones. Granite offers a selection of interesting colors, from dark green-blue through to a pinkish gray. If possible, search out salvaged pieces. You could use salvaged road setts to edge a paving circle, or pieces of quarry stone as feature stones to edge a flight of steps, and so on.

Sand and gravel

Soft sand, sometimes called builder's sand, is used for making mortar, while sharp sand is used for concrete. Locally produced sand always complements the color of the stone and brick in the area. Be wary about buying bagged sand from a distant quarry, as it will be a different color to your local stone. Gravel comes in many grades, from fine pea grit to gravel the size of a small egg. Both gravel and sand are best purchased in bulk from a local pit.

BUYING TIPS

- Make sure that sand has been washed and screened so that it doesn't contain any salt, clay, or animal or vegetable matter. Salty sand will kill your plants, weaken mortar and concrete mixes, and effervesce out of stonework and brickwork. Clay will weaken mortar and concrete mixes.
- A lorry-load of sand will always work out much cheaper than bagged sand, sometimes a quarter of the cost. The next cheapest option is to have the sand delivered by the ton in a huge bag. The supplier will use a crane to unload the bag.
- If you decide to go and collect pre-bagged sand in your car, be aware of the consequences. The dead weight will alter your steering and braking, and might well damage your springs.
- Meet the delivery lorry when it arrives with your order of sand and gravel, just in case the order is incorrect or the driver attempts to unload it in the wrong place.

CONCRETE AND MORTAR

How to mix concrete

A good mix for concrete consists of 1 part cement, 2 parts sharp sand, and 3 parts aggregate. The ingredients can be measured with a shovel or bucket. Put the sand on a board or in a wheelbarrow,

Sharp sand   *Sand and gravel*   *Cement*

How to mix mortar

To make mortar, use 1 part cement and 3 parts soft sand. Put the sand on a board or in a wheelbarrow, followed by the cement powder. Use a shovel to mix the ingredients until they are well blended, then

followed by the cement powder. Turn over the mixture with the shovel until well blended, and heap up. Dig a hole in the center, then pour in a small amount of water and gradually drag the mixture into the water. When all the cement has been mixed in, add the aggregate, followed by more water. Continue mixing, all the while adding water and turning over the heap, until you have a mixture that will hold its shape when formed into a ridge.

form into a heap. Dig a hole in the center and pour in a small quantity of water. Gradually drag the dry ingredients into the water. Continue adding water and turning the heap until you achieve a mortar with a firm, buttery consistency. A slice of mortar should stand up without crumbling. A good test is to take a dampened brick and butter one face with the mortar: it should stick and hold its shape without running.

OTHER USEFUL MATERIALS

Chicken wire makes a great anti-slip surface—buy the smallest size of mesh. Black plastic sheeting is good for holding back the growth of weeds. You can either buy the very expensive woven sheet that is specifically designed to let water drain away, or you

can simply go for the cheapest plastic that you can find, and punch it full of holes. If the sheeting is going to go under gravel or bark, you can use just about any plastic that comes to hand, such as plastic bags, old packaging, or woven plastic sacks.

Foundations

Just about every path, step, and patio starts with a foundation. But if you are under the impression that every foundation needs to be a massive concrete slab, that is not the case. There are many options, ranging from gravel to crushed stone, compacted clinker or concrete. This section tells you how to select a suitable foundation.

PATIO AND PATH FOUNDATIONS

Once you have decided on the path or patio, you need to study the site. Dig a small hole and have a good look at the ground under the topsoil. Is it hard or soft? Is there a lot of rock and rubble, or is there a layer of clay or sand? Is it wet or dry? Does water soak away swiftly, or does it sit in a puddle? Well-drained, compacted soil needs less of a foundation than more unstable areas. The options for a foundation range from a trench filled with gravel to a trench packed with compacted clinker and topped by a layer of concrete (and various combinations in between), so in the light of your survey, spend time considering your needs.

For example, when we built the Snake-pattern Cobble Path (see page 108), we found that the site was so wet and boggy that we needed to lay a concrete slab. The planned site for the Decking Tile Patio (see page 34) was covered by such a thick layer of bark chippings that we needed only the lightest of foundations— just enough to spread the load from the weight of the patio.

If the site is dry, rocky, and stable, you can get away with a thin layer of clinker and not much else. But if the site is wet, squashy, and unstable, you need to dig a trench, and half-fill it with gravel for drainage, then top it off with a generous layer of concrete. Think hard about your expectations for the project. Do you want it to last for twenty years, or are you happy for it to crumble back into the landscape after a few years? If you want it to be permanent and unshakable, a concrete slab is the answer. But if you want it to last for only a few years and don't really mind if it moves with the passing of the seasons, a layer of well-compacted clinker will do the trick. Consider the options; think hard about the time, costs, and energy required; and then make your decision.

Decorative paved surface
Tamped level on a bed of sand and gaps filled with more sand

Slabs
Set on blobs of mortar, one at each corner and one in the middle

Mortar
Slabs bedded on a layer of mortar

Edging
An optional decorative feature

Clinker
Compacted rubble at least 2 1/2 in. thick

Sand
A compacted layer of sand

Clinker
Compacted rubble at least 2 1/2 in. thick

Concrete
At least 1 1/2 in. thick, cast within a wooden frame

ABOVE **A decorative patio made of reconstituted stone slabs set on a foundation of compacted sand spread over clinker. This foundation is suitable for use on well-drained, compacted soil.**

ABOVE **For a path that will get a lot of use, slabs are set on a foundation of clinker topped with concrete, and bedded on a thin layer of mortar.**

FOUNDATIONS FOR STEPS

All steps need some sort of foundation, even if it is only a couple of concrete blocks (as with the Wooden Stairway on page 120). Under a short flight of railroad tie steps, you can get away with a foundation of just a layer of clinker because it doesn't matter too much if the steps move independently of each other. Stone steps definitely need a stable foundation that is going to stay put, and must be built on concrete. If we are constructing stone steps up a firm slope (stony ground with plenty of drainage), we start by building an extra-large foundation slab under the bottom step, which becomes the anchor for the rest of the flight of steps. First, we clear the ground under the first and second steps, put in the clinker, and then lay a concrete slab that runs back into the slope. We then build up a retaining wall for the first riser, backfill behind the riser with more clinker, and lay a thinner concrete slab in readiness for the next riser. In this way, we gradually work up the slope building the other steps.

The guiding rule to follow is this: the wetter the ground, the more clinker and the thicker the layer of concrete required for the foundation. The best way to proceed is to look at the ground, dig a small trial hole, and then take it from there.

Riser
Made of bricks and mortar

Tread
A stone paver bedded on top of the clinker

Clinker
2½ in. thickness of compacted rubble

Concrete
A cast slab at least 1½ in. thick

Clinker
Backfilled behind the riser wall

ABOVE Steps that will get a lot of traffic require a sturdy foundation of clinker and concrete built in stages from the bottom step upward. The most important part of the foundation is under the lowest step.

MAKING A FOUNDATION SLAB

Pegs
Arrange the pegs as shown so that the string crosses at the corners

Square
A square ensures 90° corners

String
Use the string to mark out the foundation

Dimensions
Check the dimensions with a tape measure

ABOVE Pegs, string, and a tape measure (a square may also be useful) are used to mark out a rectangular area of the correct size.

Concrete
The concrete mix is cast to the level of the boards

Wooden boards
The boards are used to set the level of the concrete

Pegs
Positioned on the outside of the frame

Clinker
A layer of compacted rubble

ABOVE A frame made from boards and pegs—called formwork—is used for casting a concrete foundation slab.

Every project will need a slightly different type of foundation slab, according to the configuration of the formwork and the proportions of clinker to concrete required to suit the weight of the project and the type of site. The basic procedure is given below.

Procedure for making a foundation slab

1 Use a tape measure, string, and wooden pegs to mark the outer limits of the foundation (the overall size of the slab, plus the thickness of the formwork boards, plus 4 in. all round). For example, if you want a finished concrete slab 6 ft. 6 in. square, and the formwork boards are ¾ in. thick, you need to set out a 7 ft. 4 in. square. Put two pegs at each corner, so that the string line runs around the site without a break. If the foundation is rectilinear, use a square to ensure that the corners are at right angles.

2 Slice back the turf and dig down to a depth of about 8 in. Level the base. Remove all the earth and turf from the site. Spread a 4 in. layer of clinker over the whole site, and stamp it flat with the sledgehammer. Make sure that the clinker is well compacted, with no cavities or loose areas. Pay particular attention to the edges. Build the formwork using square wooden pegs and 4 in.-wide boards. Use screws rather than nails to fix the boards to the pegs, to avoid knocking the pegs askew. Use a level to ensure that the tops of the boards are level.

3 Mix the concrete: 1 part cement, 2 parts sharp sand, and 3 parts aggregate. Pour it into the formwork and use a wooden batten to tamp it level with the top of the formwork. If the weather is hot, repeatedly spray a fine mist of water over the concrete to ensure a long curing time. If rain threatens, cover the slab with a tarpaulin.

Brickwork and stonework techniques

In many ways, the art and craft of good brickwork and stonework can be likened to building a very complex piece of Japanese woodwork. The trick is to fit the components together with the minimum of measuring and as few cuts as possible. If you do have to make a cut, the challenge is to get it right the first time around!

WORKING WITH BRICK AND STONE

A good deal of the enjoyment of working with brick and stone is derived from studying the forms and working out how best to fit them together. If you can use the various bricks and stones as you find them—they might be new, salvaged, seconds, or left over from another job—so much the better. If cutting the materials is unavoidable, study the bricks and stones to work out how they can be fitted with the minimum of cuts. Always opt for straight cuts rather than attempting intricate curves.

CUTTING BRICK AND STONE

Cutting brick and stone

Brick and stone can be cut with a traditional bolster chisel and club hammer, in which case the procedure is relatively slow and quiet, but the break is not very reliable. Alternatively, you can go for the noisy, but more certain, option of using an angle grinder.

The traditional way of cutting bricks is to hold the brick in your hand and give it a couple of hard chops with a bricklayer's trowel. But if you are a beginner, use a bolster chisel. Position the brick on a firm surface, then set the bolster chisel on the marked line and give it a well-placed blow with the club hammer. Natural and reconstituted stone can be cut in much the same way. However, the easiest method is to first score the line with the angle grinder and then use the chisel to make the final cut.

Procedure for cutting stone

1 Set the slab flat on the grass and use a tape measure, chalk, and long rule to draw the line of cut. Brace your body, hold the angle grinder so that the wheel is at right angles to the slab, and switch on the power. Set the spinning disk on the chalk line and make a light, scoring cut. Make several runs to deepen the cut, then switch off the power. Flip the slab over, and repeat the whole procedure on the other side.

2 Take the bolster chisel in one hand and the club hammer in the other, and set the edge of the chisel into the scored channel. Tap the chisel with a series of light passes, gradually increasing the power of the blows. Concentrate on the center area, rather than the edges. Continue until the stone breaks into two.

> ### CAUTION
>
> Stone-cutting is potentially very dangerous, with lots of dust and sharp splinters, so wear a dust-mask, goggles, ear defenders, strong gloves, and stout boots.

Wear thick, protective gloves

Never remove the guard

Score the paver with the cutter

ABOVE Use an angle grinder to score a deep line on both faces of the paver. Hold the grinder firmly and keep your feet out of the way.

BELOW Complete the cut by breaking the stone in two using a bolster chisel and hammer.

Keep the bolster chisel upright

LAYING PAVING SLABS

Mortar
Use a firm mixture

Joints
Ensure the gaps between the slabs are uniform

Firm, level base

ABOVE Set the slab on five blobs of mortar—one at each corner and one in the middle. Tap the slab level and do not stand on it until dry.

Start by laying a foundation. If the ground is stony and well drained, clinker topped with sand is adequate. If the ground is wet and badly drained, you need a foundation of gravel covered with clinker, topped off with concrete.

Once the foundation is in place, have a trial run and set out the slabs without mortar. See how they fit together, and check how many are required and whether or not you need to cut any of them. When you are happy with the arrangement, mix a pile of stiff mortar. Dampen the underside of a slab, then set five generous daubs of mortar on the foundation and gently bed the slab into position. Make adjustments by tapping the slab with the handle of a club hammer, and check the level by using a level.

POINTING WITH MORTAR

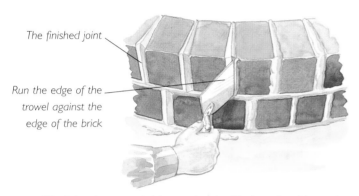

The finished joint

Run the edge of the trowel against the edge of the brick

Minimum gap of 1/2 in.

Run the edge of the trowel against the edge of the stone

ABOVE The joints between bricks need to be filled neatly with mortar. Use the edge of the trowel to wipe the mortar into the joint. Approach from both sides in order to create a peaked effect.

ABOVE When positioning crazy paving that will have the gaps filled with wet mortar, leave a minimum gap of ¹/₂ in. between each stone and preferably more (otherwise it is difficult to fill the gaps).

When you have set your bricks or stone slabs in place to make a wall, the gaps between them, or joints, need to be filled or pointed with mortar. To fill brickwork, start by using the tip of the pointing trowel to tidy up the joints as they stand. Then use the pointing trowel to spread a generous slice of fresh mortar on the face of the bricklayer's trowel. Spread the mortar until it is more or less the same thickness as the joint that you want to fill. Using the edge of the pointing trowel like a spatula, lift the mortar clear with a slicing, wiping action, so that it finishes up on the back edge of

the trowel. This movement is tricky, so you will need to practice to get it right. Push the slice of mortar into the gap with a firm, wiping action. Repeat this procedure on all the joints to be filled. Finally, wash the trowel in clean water, then tidy up the vertical and horizontal joints.

Filling a paved area is done in much the same way—the only difference is that you have to adjust the thickness of the mortar on the bricklayer's trowel, and angle your approach to suit the width and position of the joint to be filled.

GAP-FILLING PAVING SLABS WITH DRY MORTAR OR SAND

Brush the slabs to remove any stray blobs of mortar, then leave them until the mortar underneath has set and the slabs are completely dry. It's important that the paving is absolutely dry. You also need to undertake the task on a fine, sunny day, not when the weather is damp and overcast. Decide whether to fill the joints with sand or dry-mix mortar. If you decide on sand, search around for fine silver sand. The sand needs to be bone dry. If you want to use dry-mix mortar, mix a small heap in the proportions of 1 part

cement to 3 parts fine sand. Once again, it important that all the ingredients are dry. Make sure that the mixture does not contain any stones, hard lumps, or other debris.

Heap the sand or dry-mix mortar on the paving and use a soft-bristled broom to gently ease it into the joints. Run the brush in all directions until all the joints have been filled. Make sure that the surface of the slabs is free from dry-mix mortar. Wait until the day after it first rains before walking on the paving.

Woodwork techniques

Woodwork is an exciting, calming, and therapeutic activity, and for the projects in this book, you can enjoy working outside in spring and summer. Later, you can revel in showing off the completed project to your friends and family, and get pleasure from seeing how it enriches the garden. The following techniques will enable you to complete all the projects with the minimum of expertise, effort, and expense.

WORKING WITH WOOD

Don't worry if you are a raw beginner. Do not be intimidated by visions of highly finished, traditional woodwork—garden woodwork is much easier to do and altogether less hidebound, with no complex jointing procedures or necessity to plane with the grain. Of course, garden woodwork does require that you learn one or two basic techniques, but these are not difficult. If you are capable of using a saw, holding a chisel, setting a post in the ground, cutting wood to length, cutting a few basic curves, banging in nails, driving in screws, and cutting one or two joints, you are quite able to make all the projects in this book.

SETTING POSTS INTO THE GROUND

Traditionally, the below-ground section of wooden posts was charred or tarred for protection before being set in a mix of clay and rubble. Today, posts are simply purchased ready-treated with preservative, and supported in either clinker or concrete. Start by digging a hole one spade-width square and about two spade depths deep. Try to keep the hole straight-sided and as narrow as possible. If the ground is reasonably dry and well drained, set the post on a piece of old tile or brick, then check with the level that it is perfectly upright, and compact clinker around it. If the post needs a bit more support, dig the hole as already described, then set the post upright on the brick or tile, with a couple of stays and a small amount of clinker to hold it in position, and fill the hole with concrete. Leave the concrete to set overnight.

ABOVE In firm, dry soil, a post can be set in a hole and surrounded by compacted rubble. For other soil types, it is best to use concrete in addition to clinker. Lengths of wood are used to hold the post in position until the concrete has set.

CUTTING WOOD TO LENGTH

If you have bought all your wood in prepared sections in order to make the projects to exactly the dimensions described, all you need to do is cut the wood to length with straight cuts.

To make a straight cut at right angles to the face or edge of the wood (across the run of the grain), take the set square and a carpenter's pencil, and strike a line around the wood. Let's say that you want to cut 4 in. off the end of a 3 in.-square post. Hold the wooden handle of the square (sometimes known as the "stock") hard against the workpiece, and run a pencil line against the edge of the steel blade. Repeat this procedure on all faces and edges of the post until the line encircles the wood.

This done, support the workpiece on a couple of portable workbenches, with the line of cut just clear of the bench. Take the crosscut saw and position the teeth to the waste side of the drawn line, and make a few short, dragging strokes. When the saw begins to bite, use the full length of it to make the cut. Keep sighting down the saw to ensure that the blade is running true with the drawn line. When you come to within a few strokes of finishing the cut, hook your free hand under the piece of waste, or ask a helper to do so, and make lighter strokes until the wood is sawn through. On no account let the wood break off under its own weight, as it is likely to splinter.

CUTTING CURVES IN WOOD

For cutting swift, broad curves in thick wood, we favor a power jigsaw. Bridge the workpiece across a couple of workbenches, so that the area to be cut is well clear of the benches. Set the bed of the saw on the workpiece with the blade just clear of the wood. Switch on the power and slowly advance the tool so that the line of cut runs slightly to the waste side of the drawn line. When you approach the end of the cut, ease off the pressure and advance until the blade runs clear of the wood, then switch off the power. Keep your attention fixed on the saw until the blade comes to a standstill, and then remove the blade from the wood.

RIGHT Use a jigsaw for cutting curved shapes (but never use a jigsaw on round-section wood). Choose a blade type to suit the job.

Rotate the saw to make the blade follow the curve

Keep the sole of the jigsaw flat on the surface of the wood

NAILING, SCREWING AND BOLTING

Check the joint is square before putting in the second screw

Use two screws for most joints

ABOVE Use screws positioned diagonally to create a strong joint. Drill holes in the top piece of wood before screwing.

Use large washers behind the nuts

Don't over-tighten the nuts or the wood could be crushed

ABOVE Bolts make very strong joints, which are necessary in large frameworks such as those used to support decking boards.

The projects use three types of fixings for jointing wood: countersunk crossheaded screws, nails (bright steel and galvanized), and coach bolts with nuts and washers to fit. Using an electric drill, we drill holes for bolts and make pilot holes for screws. However, if the screw positions occur well away from the end of the wood, where there is little risk of the wood splitting, we sometimes drive in the screws without drilling pilot holes. We use a cordless electric screwdriver fitted with a cross-point bit. You could use a hand screwdriver, but the cordless screwdriver gets the job done faster, and the process is a lot less tiring. It's a wonderful tool for big projects with lots of parts that need to be screwed together. If you intend working over several days, remember to recharge the cordless drill overnight.

When extra strength is required, we use coach bolts for the primary joints. Measure the diameter of the bolt and drill a hole the same size through the workpiece. It is important that the shank of the bolt is a tight fit in the hole. Knock the bolt into place so that the square section on the underside of the domed head locks into the drilled hole. Slide a washer and nut on the bolt, and tighten up the nut with a ratchet wrench.

CUTTING JOINTS

Apart from butted and overlapping joints, when two or more components are set face to face and fixed with screws or bolts, the only other joint we use for the projects is the end lap. This involves lapping one component over another, and then cutting half the material away from each part so that they fit together with faces and edges flush. For example, in the Green Wood Walkway (see page 56), the floor beams are lapped end to end.

The procedure is as follows. Use the tape measure, pencil, and square to set out the size and shape of the end laps, then cut down the shoulder-line with a saw. Finally, set an ax on the mark and use a mallet to chop out the waste. If you are anxious about using the ax, you could substitute a very wide chisel instead. Whatever the cutting context, the rule is to saw across the grain and split with the run of the grain.

Paths

Paths enhance the garden in the sense that they are functionally desirable—you might need a path to cross a lawn, to mark out the quickest route, or so that you won't get your feet muddy. But paths also stimulate the imagination. A path slowly winding out of sight round a corner or through a gate in a wall or hedge can be enticing, mysterious, and inspirational—a route for your feet, eyes, and mind to follow.

BRICK AND STONE

ABOVE A brick and paver path that has the brick edging flush with the lawn to ensure easy mowing.

ABOVE A traditional chevron brick path with contrasting edge pieces, so there is no need to cut bricks.

ABOVE A brick and paver path is versatile—it can be arranged in any pattern and direction.

Consider how your garden might benefit by having one or more paths. Would a path save wear and tear on the lawn? Would a dry, clean path help keep the house free of muddy footprints? Would it make life easier if there were paths around the vegetable plots? Or perhaps a slow, meandering path would add a touch of excitement to an otherwise dull garden?

Undoubtedly, your choice of path will to a great extent depend on your requirements and your liking for certain materials, but some paths are more suited to certain situations than others. For example, a straight brick and stone path is decorative and hard-wearing, and perfect for running directly between two points. (If you have salvaged materials, such as bricks and stones

rescued from an outhouse or shed that you are pulling down, so much the better.) A zigzag brick and stone path, or a gently curved flagstone and brick path, can be employed to provide a barrier between the lawn and the flower border. Not only can you stroll along the path to admire the plants and to do the weeding, but the width of the path also prevents the grass from invading the beds. A zigzag path can be built with the minimum of planning—in fact it can be built slowly over many months or even years. You simply put down the basic module of brick and stone, and add more modules to the left and right to fit the edge of the lawn. All these paths can be built slightly lower than the level of the lawn to aid easy mowing—a really good point in their favor!

EDGINGS FOR BRICK AND STONE PATHS

Functionally, an edging stops a path from spreading; however, it can also transform a dull path into something really dynamic. For example, you could make an edging from locally gathered fieldstone, or push in a Victorian-style ceramic rope-topped edging, or set bricks on edge to create a dogtooth effect. The edging can be bold, or it can vanish away into the lawn to make mowing easier.

ABOVE There are many edgings to choose from: some are functional and others are purely decorative. From left to right: reconstituted stone coping block, rope-top edging, brick edging, shaped reconstituted stone block, various ceramic and reconstituted stone edging tiles, and a corner post. Be aware that some edgings are so expensive that they can double the cost of a length of path.

WOODEN WALKWAYS

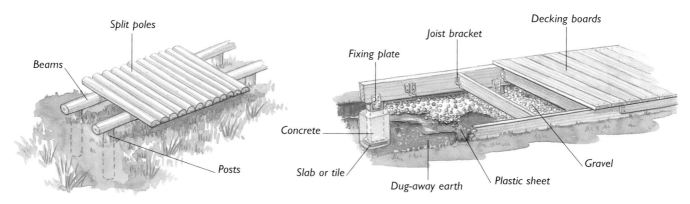

Split poles

Beams

Posts

Decking boards

Joist bracket

Fixing plate

Concrete

Slab or tile

Dug-away earth

Plastic sheet

Gravel

ABOVE This walkway is constructed from rustic poles with the bark removed. It has been built a little above ground level in order to minimize contact with wet grass and earth.

ABOVE A decking walkway suits more formal areas. Pressure-treated wood is used, and strong beams form the sides. If the ground is soft or wet, the supporting posts need to be set in concrete.

A wooden walkway is actually just a path or patio made of wood, which is usually slightly elevated from the ground. The structure can be made from green wood, sawn wood, or even from wood that has been planed and molded. It may be built on a bed of gravel, on short piles (see the Green Wood Walkway on page 56), or even built on posts (see the Raised Decking on page 114). Decking originated in frontier towns in the American West, and in Australia, where wood was relatively cheap. It was often necessary to build a level surface over bumpy, wet, or sloping ground, and decking provided a quick and cheap solution.

If you are considering building a wooden walkway, start by looking at your garden and studying the geography. Do you want the surface some considerable distance off the ground to accommodate an extremely sloping site? Or is it simply going to be built over slightly bumpy ground? If the ground is steeply sloped but stable, you will need long wooden posts concreted into holes; if it is level but wet, you could use short stub posts set in concrete with a layer of gravel covering the ground. If the land is completely level and well drained, you can bed wooden tiles directly into gravel, without the need for posts or piles.

STEPPING-STONE PATHS

Made of natural stone, concrete slabs, bricks, or wood, the good thing about stepping-stone paths is that they can be put down with the minimum of fuss and disturbance. They are also great performers when it comes to mowing the lawn—you don't have to worry about mowing around the stones, you simply ignore them. Esthetically, stepping-stones meandering across a lawn give the appearance of stony outcrops, while a path made up of sawn tree rounds, set in gravel or bark, looks beautifully at home in a wooded garden. Over time, a stepping-stone path will merge attractively into the landscape, as it gradually gets partially covered with grass, moss, and fallen leaves.

Procedure for making a stepping-stone path
1 Space out the stones across your lawn. When you have achieved a good arrangement—which suits the length of your stride and complements the surrounding garden—dig around the stones with a spade and lift them to one side. Remove the turf and earth to a depth of 8 in. Clear the turf and earth from the site.
2 Spread a 3 ½ in.-thick layer of sand in the recess and carefully ease and bed the stone in place. Adjust the sand until the stone is level and slightly lower than the lawn. Use a hammer and a short beam of wood to wedge the stone into the underlying sand.

ABOVE These cleverly shaped decking tiles are a quick way to create a wiggly path and are an option for a well-drained modern garden.

Dig around each stone individually

Level the stones using sand

ABOVE Space natural stones to match the size of your stride. Bed the stones on a layer of sand so that they are at the same level as the grass—this will make it easy to mow the lawn.

Patios

Create a dynamic focal point in your garden by building a patio. This versatile area provides somewhere to put a table and chairs; a dry, level place for children to play; a site for the barbecue; or a spot to laze on a lounger. The options available are almost limitless—for example, stone, wood, decorative combinations of materials, split-level decking, or decorative kits. Make your own selection to complement the style of your garden.

BRICK AND STONE PATIOS

Pavers
Natural or reconstituted stone

Bricks

Setts

Bricks
Arranged in a pattern

ABOVE A classic-style patio made from bricks and pavers in a random decorative pattern. This design makes possible interspersed areas of planting, which are useful for injecting interest into large paved areas.

ABOVE A small, circular patio has the potential to transform a tiny garden, adding pattern and texture.

If you live in an area where the weather is damp for a good part of the year, and your garden consists of a lawn surrounded by lots of foliage, a traditional brick or stone patio will enable you to get more use out of the garden. This type of patio will last forever.

Procedure for making a brick and stone patio

1 Mark out the size of the patio with a tape measure and string. Remove all the turf and earth to a depth of about 8 in. Rake a 4-in. layer of ballast over the bottom of the recess. Spread a thin layer of sand over the ballast and tamp it smooth with a tamping beam. Repeat this several times, until the sand is well compacted and within 2¾ in. of the level of the lawn.

2 Set the modules of brick and stone on generous blobs of mortar, easing them until the mortar is slightly displaced and the faces of the bricks and stones are more or less level with the lawn. Tamp the arrangement with the beam and a club hammer. Check with the level and make corrections until the bricks and stones are level. Re-run this procedure for all the modules. Make sure that the various joints are staggered.

3 When all the bricks and stones are in position, leave them overnight until the mortar has set. Wait for a sunny day and then shovel a mixture of sand and grass seed over the whole patio, before using a bass broom to sweep it into all the joints. Finally, spray a thin mist of water over the patio to dampen the mixture.

EDGING FOR BRICK AND STONE PATIOS

If, when you are digging away the turf and earth for a patio, you see that the ground is wet and spongy, it would be wise to add an edging to stop the patio from spreading. You have a choice between an above-surface edging such as bricks or tiles, which will frame the whole arrangement like a picture frame, or a below-surface edging that does the job but more or less vanishes from view. Edgings can also be used purely for decorative effect.

For example, with the brick and stone patio described above, the outer bricks or stones could themselves become the edging. At the edges of the patio, replace the layers of ballast, sand, and mortar with a concrete footing. In this way, the outermost bricks and stones become a containing ring, like a kerb. If you want a further edging to stand proud, dig a trench around the outermost bricks, then fill with a little clinker and bed the edging in mortar.

DECKING PATIO

LEFT Decking patios can be shaped to suit your needs. It is not difficult to create L-shapes and angled sides (try to avoid curves). ABOVE Decking boards can be arranged to make patterns, but make sure that the ends of the decking are supported by joists beneath.

Decking patios are the perfect solution when you want to build a patio on a sloping site without going to the trouble of laying a huge foundation slab. They can be used to link the house to the garden. Decking enables you to achieve a level surface without building walls. It is rather like a massive table, with the legs of the table designed to suit the slope of the land, and steps built to run up to the level surface. This system works whatever the lay of the land, but the most dramatic results are seen if the site is really sloping, falling sharply away from the house. The structure is built in much the same way as the upper level of a house, with a framework of joists covered by a layer of boards to make a floor.

Procedure for making a patio on a sloping site

1 Use a tape measure, pegs, and string to mark out the shape and size of the patio. Decide on the position of the main support posts and the spacing of the joists in relation to the shape of the patio and the thickness of the floorboards. Dig holes and set the posts in concrete. Use a tape measure and level to establish the height and level of the platform. Nail temporary battens from post to post, to ensure that they remain upright.

2 Screw the outer ring of primary joists to the posts and infill with the pattern of secondary joists.

Decide how you want the floorboards to meet the outer joists. Do you want to cut the ends flush and trim them with a molded batten? Or do you want the ends to overhang like the surface of a table? Sit down with a pencil and paper and draw out your ideas before you start cutting wood.

Run the floorboards across the joists and fix them in place with two screws for each board–joist intersection. Space the boards about $1/2$ in. apart to leave room for expansion.

DECORATIVE PATIO KITS

It is possible to buy small patios in kit form. There are circular reconstituted stone kits that look like granite stone setts, cut flagstones, or bricks; kits that contain a mixture of brick and stone; circular decking kits that unroll like a carpet; and many other patterns, shapes, and materials. Kits are undoubtedly a more expensive option than buying a heap of basic materials and building your own design, but they are a good choice if you want a quick, small patio with a complex pattern. One such kit comes complete with various numbered blocks and a large paper pattern. The pattern is positioned on the concrete slab, and the numbered blocks are set in place on the pattern. A dry mix of concrete and sand is then swept over the patio to fill the joints.

RIGHT These reconstituted stone setts are tesselating modules, which enable various shapes and sizes of patio to be covered with circular patterns. Cobbles arranged by hand complete the design.

Steps

If you have a sloping garden, there are two ways of moving from one level to another. You can scramble up and down the slope and hope that you don't slip, or you can build one or more flights of steps. Apart from being a practical solution, steps can also function as a feature that leads the eye from one level to another.

BRICK AND STONE STEPS

Contrasting stone sides

Soldier bricks

"Crazy"-paved tread

Flagstone tread

Brick riser

Slope of ground

Clinker and gravel backfill

Clinker

Concrete slab

ABOVE Steps with brick risers, "crazy"-paved treads, and contrasting stone sides. The traditional soldier brick edge to the steps is an attractive detail. The "crazy" paving could be replaced by gravel.

Garden steps can of course be made solely from brick or stone, but they are commonly made from a mix of both materials. Bricks are good for building risers and stone slabs are good for building treads, and the two forms and textures complement each other. Salvaged materials are perfect for the job. Ideally, the riser needs to be between 6–8 in. high, while the tread needs to measure between 12–16 in. from front to back.

Procedure for building steps from "crazy" paving and soldier bricks

1 Use a tape measure, pegs, and string to establish the size and position of the steps on the ground. Lay a generous concrete slab foundation (at ground level), to run under the first riser, the first tread, and second riser.
2 Build up brickwork to form the first step, making it two bricks high, with the top line made from soldier bricks set so that the heads look toward the front of the step.
3 When the mortar has cured, backfill behind the first riser wall with compacted clinker topped off with gravel. Lay the "crazy"-paving slabs on blobs of mortar to make the first tread. Check with a level. Build a second riser wall off

---

| **USEFUL TIP** |

If you have trouble visualizing the finished steps, build a full-size mock-up of a single step, so that you can see how the steps are going to look in terms of size and texture.

ABOVE The whole flight of steps is supported on the concrete foundation slab under the first (bottom) step. The treads are single, natural stone pavers but could be replaced with reconstituted pavers.

the back of the first tread, and continue as just described. Repeat the process for the whole flight of steps. If there are more than six steps, build a foundation slab for every seventh step.

Procedure for building brick and flagstone steps

1 Use a tape measure, pegs, and string to set out the size and position of the flight of steps on the ground. Remove the turf and earth—so that you have a cut trench running up the sloping ground—and lay a concrete foundation slab at ground level to run under the first riser, the first tread, and second riser.
2 Build up brickwork to form the first riser, making it two bricks high, with the best face looking toward the front of the step. Make checks with the level.
3 When the mortar has cured, backfill behind the first riser wall with compacted clinker topped off with gravel. Butter the top of the bricks with mortar, then trowel blobs of mortar on the clinker, and set the flagstone in position with the nosing overhanging the riser wall. Check that it is level by using the level. Build a second riser wall off the back of the slab, and continue as already described. Repeat this procedure for the whole flight of steps.

RAILROAD TIE STEPS

Salvaged railroad ties make informal, low-rise steps which look very good in the garden. They are a handy size, measuring about 10 in. wide and 6 in. thick, relatively swift and easy to position, and virtually indestructible. (Avoid ties that exude tar or oil.) All you do is set the first tie in place and bang in posts to stop it moving forward. Next, earth is dug from the slope and compacted behind the retaining tie to make a level terrace, and so on up the slope. Finally, when all the ties are in place, you can tidy up the edge of the steps with a rockery edging, and create a tread surface with a material such as compacted stone chips.

RIGHT A design for large-scale, informal steps using railroad ties and gravel. Arrange the ties as shown to make steps that are 6 in. high and as wide as you choose.

Posts
Short lengths of tie

Clinker

Gravel infill
The width of the treads
can vary to suit the slope

EDGINGS FOR STEPS

There are two types of step—those that are cut into a slope, and those that are freestanding. There are two common solutions to edging steps. If the steps are cut into a grass bank and made of brick, stone, or railroad ties, the bank itself can form the edging. If the steps are freestanding and made of brick or stone, the edging might be made of brick, stone, or wood. For example, you could use a row of vertical logs, like a palisade. Or you could start by building brick or stone walls and then infill with the steps. You could build the flight of steps as already described in previous sections, and then build a dwarf wall off the treads. Or, easiest of all, you could pile random boulders or slabs of rough-cut stone to the side of the finished steps to make a rockery.

DECKING STEPS AND STAIRWAYS

Fixing bracket

Treads
Two decking boards

Stringer

Paver platform

Decking boards

Riser
Formed by the framework for the decking boards

ABOVE A simple design using very wide boards for the stringers (sides). The stringers can be bought ready-made and cut to length.
RIGHT Overlapped areas of decking can be used to form a series of broad steps or landings. The arrangement will depend on the site.

There are sometimes lots of local building regulations concerning the building of steps. If you are planning to build a flight of more than two steps, talk to the planning department and see what they recommend. There are many options: for a short flight of two treads, you can have a simple arrangement with two stringers (side boards) and treads. If the flight is higher than two treads, then for safety's sake, you also need posts and railings. If the decking is intended for family use, ideally you need a wide stairway complete with deep (front to back) and shallow (in height) steps, risers, posts, and baluster rails. If you don't like the idea of a long flight of stairs running from one level to another, you can either replace the steps with a cascade of narrow decking landings, or you can break up the flight with a series of landings. To finish the wood, opt for a flat preservative rather than an enamel varnish.

Part 2: **Projects**

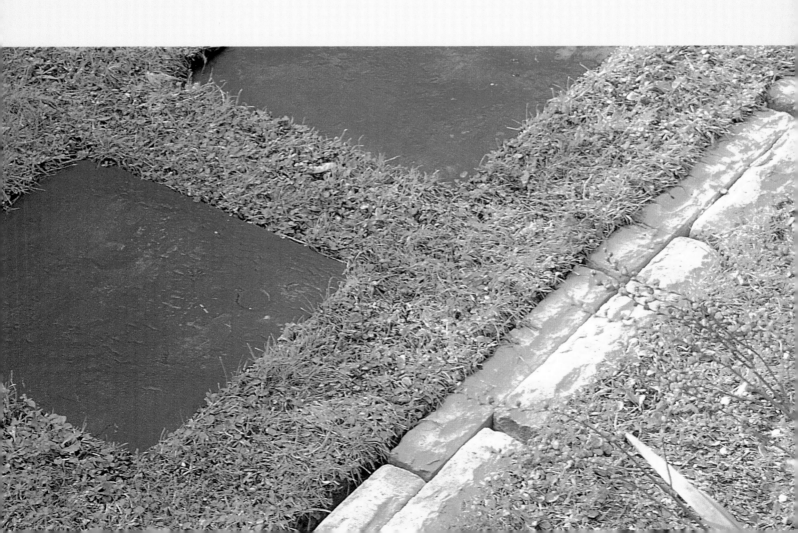

Decking tile patio

Decking tiles are a great idea. They will transform a patch of lawn or a scruffy old concrete patio into a smart, user-friendly seating area, which is perfect for entertaining or just for enjoying the sun. If you are looking for a relatively inexpensive way of creating an instant patio, decking tiles are the answer.

TIME

A single day (about six hours for all the measuring, cutting, and spreading, and the rest of the time for positioning the tiles).

SPECIAL TIP

When choosing your wood, make sure that it is straight grained and free from faults. Buy wood that has been treated with preservatives.

YOU WILL NEED

Materials *for a patio 8 ft. 8 in. square*
- Pine: 4 rough-sawn pieces, 8 ft. 8 in. long, 3 in. square section (frame)
- Decking tiles: 160 pieces, 24 in. long, 3 in. wide, and ¾ in. thick.
- Doweling: 1 piece, 12 in. long and ⅜ in. in diameter
- Plastic sheet: 1 piece, 8 ft. 4 in. square
- Gravel: 1 bucketful of medium-sized gravel per tile
- Builder's or soft sand: 1 bucketful per tile
- Galvanized nails: 9 lb. 1⅜ in. long

Tools
- Pencil, rule, tape measure, and square
- Two portable workbenches
- Crosscut saw
- Ax or wide chisel
- Mallet
- Electric drill with a ⅜ in. flat bit
- Shovel
- Rake
- Club hammer
- Tamping beam: about 20 in. long

ALL SQUARE AND SHIPSHAPE

The wonderful thing about this project is that it can be done quickly. You don't have the problem of digging foundations—the whole idea is that you can set the decking on an existing surface without too much preparation. Whether you are going to lay the tiles on an old concrete patio, uneven "crazy" paving, or a squashy patch of chipped bark, you simply put down the frame and unroll the plastic, then spread the gravel and sand, and lay the tiles. If you want a much larger patio, just increase the quantities accordingly.

To make a tile, cut 10 x 24 in. lengths of 3-in. wide wood and set them in position—seven on top and three underneath, and all spaced as shown—and fix them with nails.

DETAIL OF THE DECKING TILE PATIO

Decking tile
made from 10 lengths of wood, each 24 in. x 3 in. x ¾ in.

Gravel

Plastic

Frame
8 ft. 8 in. x 3 in. x 3 in.

Sand

End lap joint
3 in. long, 1½ in. deep, ⅜ in. hole in the middle

Step-by-step: **Making the decking tile patio**

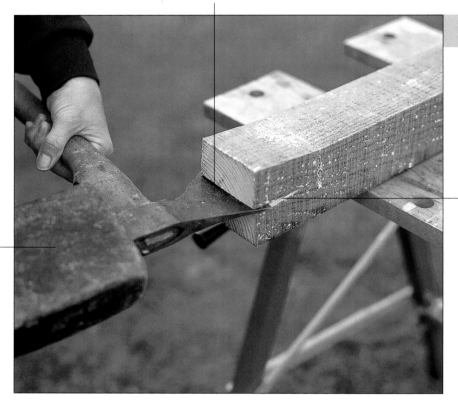

Ax
Hold the ax so that the blade is square with the wood

Mallet
Give the ax a series of taps

Grain
Maneuver the ax so that the split runs along the grain

1 Take the four 8 ft. 8 in. lengths of 3 in. square-section wood and use the tape measure, pencil, and square to set out the end laps at the ends, making them 1½ in. deep and 3 in. long. Saw down the shoulder-line, and then use the ax and mallet to chop out the waste.

Alignment
Make sure that the two pieces of wood are at 90° to each other

2 Set the frame together, carefully squaring and aligning the end laps. Drill through the center of the corner joints with the ⅜ in. drill bit. Tap a piece of dowel, 3 in. long, through each joint.

Helpful hint

When drilling through the joint, sight down the drill so that the hole runs through the wood at right angles to the face. Ease off the pressure as the bit exits to prevent the wood from splitting.

Drainage
*Spike a few holes in the plastic
to let the patio drain freely*

Plastic
*Tuck the
plastic sheet
well under
the wood*

Raking
*Level the gravel
and cover with
a layer of sand.
It should reach
to just below
the top of the
frame*

3 Spread the plastic sheet over the site. Position the frame squarely on it, so that the edges of the plastic are covered. Rake a thin layer of gravel over the plastic sheet, and top it off with a layer of sand, filling the frame to just below the top.

Tamping
*Tap the beam
with the
hammer until
the tile is level
with the top of
the frame*

4 Gently ease the tiles into position. Finally, use the club hammer and tamping beam to bed the tiles into the sand, ensuring that they are level with each other and with the frame.

Helpful hint

When ordering decking tiles, specify ones that have been treated with preservative. Avoid tiles with areas of mold, splits, or other damage. Some suppliers store materials outside—if so, check that the tiles have not suffered as a result.

Zigzag brick border path

Bricks make a most attractive path, which is perfect for edging a lawn and visually blending it into the flower borders, and is sturdy enough to cope with a wheelbarrow being pushed up and down it. An added advantage of this type of path is that it lets the edge of the lawn be mowed easily—you just ignore the path and mow over it.

TIME

One day for a 32-brick path.

SPECIAL TIP

Brick prices vary hugely. We halved our costs by using seconds, which are perfectly suitable for the task.

PERSPECTIVE VIEW OF THE ZIGZAG BRICK BORDER PATH

Flower border

Brick level
The bricks are level with the lawn or slightly lower

Brick
*8 in. x 3³⁄₈ in.
Color to suit*

Sand
Thin layer of sand compacted to within 2³⁄₄ in. of lawn level

Lawn

Joint
Gap filled with sand

Brick pattern
Arranged with equal gaps

Ballast
4 in. deep

Earth
Excavated to a depth of 8 in.

YOU WILL NEED

Materials *for a path made from 4 modules of brick pattern, 20 in. square*

- Bricks: 32 bricks, 8 in. long, 3³⁄₈ in. wide, and 2¹⁄₄ in. thick (color and texture to suit your needs)
- Builder's or soft sand: about 1 bucketful per 8-brick square
- Ballast: about 1 bucketful per 8-brick square

Tools
- Spade
- Fork
- Wheelbarrow
- Shovel
- Rake
- Tamping beam: about 18 in. long, ³⁄₄ in. thick, and 4 in. wide
- Club hammer
- Brush

ZIGZAGGING ABOUT THE GARDEN

Wander round your garden and imagine how, by building zigzag brick paths, you could both tidy up the border edgings and simplify the mowing of the lawn. The design is based on an 8 in. square made of two bricks, four of which are placed together to make a larger 16¹⁄₂ in. square. By taking this 16¹⁄₂ in. square as the basic module, it is possible to free-flow the squares together to create the characteristic zigzag design. The great thing about this technique is that you don't have to use a tape measure—you simply set the bricks directly on the ground.

We have cut costs by using seconds, but you can also economize by using old bricks, such as those salvaged from a building site. Position the bricks with the frog, or depression, on the underside. Avoid bricks that show cracks or holes.

Step-by-step: Making the zigzag brick border path

Alignment
Sight down the row of bricks
to ensure that they are in line

Design
Take time
arranging the
bricks to your
satisfaction

1 Arrange the bricks so that they bleed into the flower border from the lawn. When you have achieved a pleasing design, carefully cut around the path shape with a sharp spade.

Marking
Use the spade
to mark around
the edges of
the bricks

2 One or two modules at a time, remove the turf and earth to a depth of about 8 in. Spread and rake a 4 in. layer of ballast over the bottom of the recess.

Raking
Use the
head of the
rake to
tamp the
ballast into
place

Ballast
Be generous
with the ballast,
to avoid cavities

Sand
Always use sand that has been
washed and is free from salt

Leveling
Level the bricks, both with each
other and the surrounding lawn

Tamping
Tamp the
square in both
directions

Checking
Stand back
to check that
your layout of
bricks is good

Gloves
Wear gloves
to give you a
better grip
and to protect
your hands

3 Spread a thin layer of sand over the ballast and tamp it smooth with the beam. Repeat this several times, until the sand is well compacted and rises to within 2¾ in. of the level of the lawn.

4 Position the bricks, bedding them lightly into the sand until they are level with the lawn and each other. Space the bricks to leave a generous joint between them for filling with sand.

5 When all the bricks have been laid, tamp them level with the beam and club hammer. Finally, brush sand in and around the bricks until the whole arrangement feels firm and stable.

Tamping
Apply even
pressure across
several bricks
to bring them
level without
breaking them

Helpful hint

If you have difficulty brushing the dry sand into the joints between the bricks, use a hose to spray a fine mist of water over the whole arrangement so that the sand is washed into the gaps.

Woodland steps

These slow-rise steps are perfect for a gently sloping area. The green wood posts and poles, covered with bark, bring a touch of woodland atmosphere into your garden. You can imagine that, just hidden from view, there is a lush green forest glade waiting to be discovered. Chipped bark scattered on the treads contributes to the picture.

YOU WILL NEED

Materials *for a flight of steps about 7 ft. long, and 10 ft. wide narrowing to 7 ft.*
(Apart from skinned and pointed poles, green wood is commonly sold to the nearest foot length.)
- Green wood: 13 posts, 3 ft. long and 6 in. in diameter (to be cut in half for the 26 flanking piles)
- Green wood: 3 posts, 7 ft. long and 3 in. in diameter (treads)
- Green wood: 1 post, 10 ft. long and 3 in. in diameter (top tread)
- Green wood: 8 pointed poles, 12–20 in. long and 2 in. in diameter (tread supports)

- Plastic sheet: 20 ft. long and 40 in. wide
- Gravel or ballast: 1 wheelbarrow load for each step
- Chipped bark: 1 wheelbarrow load for each step

Tools
- Crosscut saw
- Small ax
- Tape measure, pegs, and string
- Spade
- Fork
- Wheelbarrow
- Sledgehammer
- Scissors

A WILD WALK

This project neatly solves the tricky problem of how to build steps without going to all the trouble of digging footings, mixing concrete, and so on. To start, a narrow walkway is edged with green wood posts, and then the area within it is terraced. The building procedure is beautifully simple. The shape and width of the whole flight of steps is marked out on the ground, trenches are dug at the sides, and the flanking piles are positioned.

Tread posts are held in place by tread supports, which are banged into the ground until just lower than the tread. Each step consists of gravel and bark. If you want to make the flight of steps wider, or increase the number of steps, the project can be modified. It is possible to increase the depth of the steps from front to back, but the height of the risers needs to stay about the same.

PERSPECTIVE VIEW OF THE WOODLAND STEPS

Top tread
Green wood post
10 ft. x 3 in.
in diameter

Chipped bark

Tread
Green wood post
7 ft. x 3 in.
in diameter

Tread support
12–20 in. long x 2 in.
in diameter
Holds the tread in place

Flanking piles
Green wood posts
20 in. x 6 in.
in diameter

Sloping site

Gravel or ballast

Plastic sheet
20 ft. x 40 in.
To prevent weeds growing

Flanking trench
10 in. deep
Topped up with gravel

Step-by-step: **Making the woodland steps**

Pile height
*Go for a slightly
staggered arrangement*

Flanking trench
*Dig the
narrowest
possible trench
—no more
than the width
of the spade*

Flanking pile
*Try to get at
least half the
length of the
pile set in
the ground*

1 Cut all the wood to length with the saw and ax. Use the tape measure, string, and pegs to set out the two flanking trenches. Remove the turf and dig out the trenches to a depth of about 10 in., keeping them as narrow as possible. Use the sledgehammer to knock the flanking piles into position.

Plastic sheet
*Spike holes
in the plastic
to enable
drainage*

2 Set the bottom tread in position and hammer in two tread supports with the sledgehammer. Position the second tread. Level the step with the sledgehammer. Cover with plastic sheet and lay down a layer of gravel and a layer of bark.

Helpful hint

If you are trying to cut costs, you can use scraps of plastic rather than new sheets. It does not matter what color it is, as long as it is strong. Suppliers may be happy to let you have some old delivery bags.

Sledgehammer
Choose one that you
can lift easily

3 Continue up the slope, positioning and fixing the treads, and spreading the plastic, gravel, and chipped bark, all the while using the sledgehammer to tamp the steps level.

Chipped bark
The bark can
be mixed with
wood chippings

Treads
Arrange the
poles so there
are no peaked
areas of wood
on the upper
surface

Sledgehammer
Always let the weight of the
sledgehammer do the work

Tread supports
The supports are slightly
lower than the treads

Alignment
Try to get the
piles upright

Gravel
Compact the
gravel into the
trench around
the base of
the piles

Bark
As the bark
settles, top it
up if necessary

4 Top up the flanking trenches with the remaining gravel (the trench to the lawn side of the posts) and tamp it level with the sledgehammer. Make sure the piles are upright and firmly in place.

5 Use the weight of the sledgehammer to stamp the bark on each step level with its tread post. Aim for a smooth, compacted finish. The finished steps form a series of shallow terraces.

Rustic log ring path

Log rings sawn from a tree make an enchantingly rustic country path, which is perfect for a damp woodland setting. The meandering log rings, gravel, and log roll edging harmonize beautifully with moist, lush borders. This path will complement any informal areas of garden, or blend naturally into a cottage-style garden.

TIME
Five hours (about an hour for each log ring).

SPECIAL TIPS
Ask your local woodland timber specialist for advice. It is best to buy a long-lasting wood such as oak or elm.

CROSS-SECTION OF THE RUSTIC LOG RING PATH

Ground level

Gravel

Chicken wire
Small mesh, 40 in. square

Trench
9 in. below ground level

Gravel recess
5 in. below ground level

Log recess
13 in. below ground level

Log ring
20 in. in diameter, 12 in. thick

Plastic sheeting
13 ft. 6 in. x 40 in.

Log roll edging
13 ft. 6 in. long x 12 in. high

YOU WILL NEED

Materials *for a path about 13 ft. 6 in. long*
- Log rings: 5 rings or slices about 20 in. in diameter and 12 in. thick (path)
- Log roll edging: 27 ft. long and about 12 in. high
- Plastic sheeting: 13 ft. 6 in. long and 40 in. wide
- Chicken wire: small-size mesh, about 9¼ sq. ft. for each log ring
- Gravel: about 2 wheelbarrow loads of washed gravel for each log slice
- Galvanized fencing staples: 2 lb. 4 oz. of ¾ in.-long staples

Tools
- Tape measure, pegs, and a string line
- Spade
- Club hammer
- Wheelbarrow
- Snap-blade knife
- Claw hammer
- Rake

LOG RING AROUND THE ROSES

If you are planning a rustic-style path, a log ring design is hard to beat. Not only does the path blend in with the borders and lawn right from the start, but as the log rings become covered with fungi and moss, the path begins to melt into the landscape.

When you have worked out the route of the path, see if you need to make any changes to the design and quantities. For example, do you want a much longer path? Or do you need to change the spacing of the log rings to suit the length of your stride? When it comes to choosing the log rings, it does not matter if they are different sizes and odd shapes, or even if they vary greatly in thickness from one to another, as long as each slice has one sound, level face. There are alternatives to using natural log rings, such as groups of smaller-diameter logs, cast concrete "logs," or short lengths of railroad tie. Decorative or colored gravel could be substituted for the natural type we have used.

The chicken wire used to cover the log rings provides a non-slip surface. It is folded and stapled to the log ring before it is put in place. When the path is completed and has settled, it's a good idea to fix the chicken wire with additional staples.

Step-by-step: **Making the rustic log ring path**

Log roll
Try to arrange in a
smooth line

1 Map out the course of the path with the tape measure, pegs and string. Dig a trench (the width of a spade and 11 in. deep) on each side of the path. Set the log roll edging in it, with the decorative side facing the path. The top should extend 1 in. above ground level.

Depth
Use the club hammer to knock the log roll into place, so that 1 in. stands proud of ground level

Earth
Push earth into the trench on the flower border side and compact it to hold the log roll in place

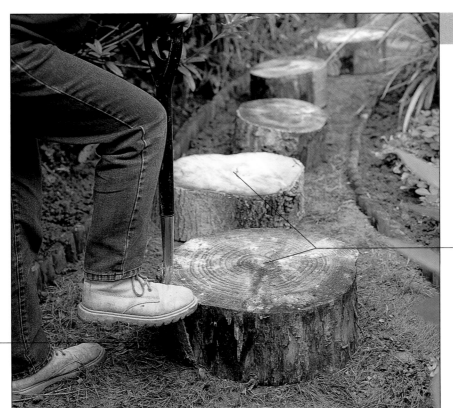

2 Position the log rings along the course of the path, spacing them to suit your stride. Dig round each log ring and remove the turf. Clear the earth to create a log recess 13 in. deep. Excavate the rest of the path to make a gravel recess 5 in. deep. (See diagram on page 46—measurements given represent the depth below ground level.)

Digging
Use the spade to chop around the shape of the log rings

Log spacing
Spend time making sure that the log rings are suitably positioned

Knife
Use an old knife to cut the plastic, because the earth will damage it

Gloves
Wear gloves to protect your hands from the wire

Plastic sheet
You could cut costs by using scraps of salvaged plastic

Chicken wire
This prevents the surface of the logs from becoming slippery

Log ring
Remember to place the log with its upper face against the wire

3 Cover the whole width of the path with plastic sheet. Slash the sheet with the knife so that you can see the recesses for the log rings. Fold the slashed plastic down into the recesses. Make sure that there is plenty of room for the logs to fall through into the recesses.

4 Cover each log ring with chicken wire, tucking and folding it on the underside, and fix it in place with the claw hammer and staples. Fix the whole log parcel with enough staples to ensure that the wire on the upper face of the log is tight and smooth.

5 Set the log rings in position, bedding them down with the club hammer until they are stable and level. Finally, spread and rake a generous layer of gravel over the plastic, but leave the log rings standing proud.

Gravel
When the ground has settled after a few days, you may need to make adjustments to the level of the gravel

Helpful hint

After a week or two, the ground will settle and both gravel and log rings may become uneven. If this happens, rake the gravel away from the log ring, lift it out, and put some gravel in the bottom of the hole. Replace the log and twist it level. Rake the gravel back around the edges.

Inspirations: Paths

Paths can be uniquely beautiful garden features. They are by their very nature a practical neccessity—perhaps a path from the front door to the gate or from the back door to the vegetable patch—but they can also inject pattern, color, and form into the garden. Many exciting effects can be created by using an imaginative combination of materials such as stone, brick, wood, cobbles, tiles, mosaic, or decorative gravels, and giving careful thought to the surrounding planting.

RIGHT The beautifully designed paths in this country garden are an interesting contrast with the rugged countryside beyond.

ABOVE The low hedge encompassing this traditional brick path gives the feeling that this is a very private garden. En route to the bower seat, a radiating pattern of random bricks encourages you to pause and admire the plants.

RIGHT (INSET) Stepping-stone paths and areas of gravel require little maintenance and complement an informal setting.

Natural patio

A quick yet eye-catching patio can be created by simply placing a geometric arrangement of flagstone slabs in the lawn, achieving a pleasing counterbalance between the stone and the grass. The spacing of the stones plumps up the grass between them to create a uniquely sumptuous, cushion-like effect.

TIME

Four hours (for nine flagstones).

SPECIAL TIP

Setting out the position of the flagstones is all-important, so don't rush the measuring-out stage.

YOU WILL NEED

Materials *for a patio 8 ft. square*
- Flagstones: 9 concrete or natural flags, 18 in. square and 2 in. thick, slate gray
- Edging stones: 44 reconstituted stone blocks, 18 in. long, 6 in. wide, and $2^5/8$ in. thick, buff color with a natural edge (sunken edging)
- Builder's or soft sand: about 1 bucketful of sand per flagstone

Tools
- Wheelbarrow
- Tape measure
- Ball of twine and 16 pegs
- Spade
- Gardening trowel
- Bolster chisel
- Club hammer
- Fork

FAIR AND SQUARE

If you are looking for a patio project that involves the minimum of expertise, cost, and work, yet you want to create a really stunning garden feature, this is the one to choose. It is designed to be set directly into an existing lawn, so you can have an instant, hard-wearing patio area without the need for clinker and concrete. When the lawn needs mowing, you can run the lawnmower straight over the slabs without a problem.

The success of the design hinges on the relationship between the size of the slabs and the width of the grass between them, which achieves a plump, springy appearance. If the slabs were any wider apart, they would be mere stepping stones, while if they were any closer, the strips of grass would be insignificant.

Instead of using the patio as a seating area, you could use it as a unique design feature by placing a continually changing selection of plants in attractive pots on the slabs.

PERSPECTIVE VIEW OF THE NATURAL PATIO

Flagstone
18 in. square,
2 in. thick
Concrete or
natural flags
in slate gray

Edging stone
18 in. x
6 in. x $2^5/8$ in.
Reconstituted
stone blocks,
buff color,
natural-finish edge

Grass
8 in. wide

*Stones are
flush with lawn*

Sand
2 in. below the level
of the lawn

Trench
6 in. deep,
$5^1/4$ in. wide

Step-by-step: **Making the natural patio**

Measuring
The success of the project hinges on careful measuring

Squaring
It is vital that the slabs are square to each other

1 Lay out the flagstones and edging stones in the proposed position on the lawn. See how the arrangement looks in relation to the overall garden design.

Edging stones
Put some edging stones side by side to check the width of the trench that will be required

Checking
Double-check all the measurements before you make cuts in the grass

Digging
Hold the spade upright to cut accurate trenches

Right angles
Make sure that the slabs are square with the edging

Pegs
The pegs are positioned back from the corners

Waste earth
Remove the excavated earth from the site so that it does not spoil the grass

2 Having made sure that the slabs are 8 in. apart and square with each other, use the pegs and twine to set out the trench for the edging. The lines of string should be 5¼ in. apart and set 8 in away from the slabs.

3 Dig out the trench with the spade and trowel, making it 6 in. deep and 5¼ in. wide. Do your best to keep the trench crisp and clean-sided, and avoid damaging the grass. Remove debris from the site in the wheelbarrow.

Level
Set the stones ever so
slightly lower than the lawn

Corners
Stagger the
stones so
that the joints
are offset

4 Set the edging stones end to end in the trench, so that the top face is flush with the level of the lawn. (To cut the stones, set the bolster chisel on the mark and give it a smart blow with the club hammer.)

Helpful hint

Do your best to keep the site clear of earth and debris. To this end, try to work on dry days, and avoid trickling earth over the grass. You might also consider standing on work boards to protect the grass, and wiping your shoes to remove mud.

Crisp cut
Aim for clean-
sided holes

5 To fit the flagstones, slice around the slab with the spade, then remove the turf with the fork and dig out a recess to a depth of about 2¼ in. Spread sand over the base of the recess and carefully bed the slab in position, so that it is level with the lawn. Repeat this procedure for all the slabs.

Sand
Spread a layer
of sand in the
hole. Make it
thick enough to
bring the slab
up to the level
of the lawn

Green wood walkway

A green wood walkway is not only a practical solution to how best to run a path over boggy, wet ground, but it is also an exciting and dynamic structure, rather like a bridge or a seaside pier. And, just like a seaside pier, you will find that the walkway soon becomes a focus and an attraction in its own right.

YOU WILL NEED

Materials *for a walkway about 9 ft. long and 3 ft. wide. (Apart from skinned and pointed poles, green wood is commonly sold to the nearest foot length.)*

- Green wood:
  30 skinned posts, 6 ft. 6 in. long and 3 in. in diameter (all the component parts)
- Galvanized chicken wire:
  10 ft. long and 40 in. wide (to make an anti-slip surface on the walkway)
- Steel nails: 7 lb. of 6 in. x ¼ in.

- Galvanized fencing staples:
  1 lb. 2 oz of ¾ in.-long staples (for fixing the chicken wire)

Tools
- Tape measure, pegs, and string
- Sledgehammer
- Level
- Portable workbench
- Crosscut saw
- Ax
- Wooden mallet
- Cordless electric drill with a drill bit to match the nail size
- Claw hammer

AN ABSOLUTE WALKOVER

You might think that a raised walkway is not very exciting, but it is in fact a most exhilarating structure both to build and to use. We found that the moment the walkway was completed, it immediately invited attention. Children started playing on it, aged relations liked the fact that it was level with a good handrail, young friends seemed to want to test out its strength, and even our dogs and cats appreciated it as a place to enjoy the sun. The building process is straightforward because there are no complicated joints to cut—instead, identical green wood round sections are sawn and nailed to each other. For bridging a patch of damp ground or perhaps a bumpy area, this is a good project to choose if you would like a structure that is a little out of the ordinary.

If the ground levels at each end of the proposed walkway are wildly different, it may be necessary to have a step at one end. If you want the walkway to go round a corner, simply build a second walkway that leads at right angles from the first, rather than attempting to incorporate a gradual bend.

To ensure that the completed walkway has a long life, it's a good idea to give the whole structure a coat of general wood preservative in the color of your choice.

CROSS-SECTION OF THE
GREEN WOOD WALKWAY

Handrail
Positioned 37 in. above the surface of the walkway

Rail support post
Green wood posts 2¾ in. in diameter are used to build the whole structure, which is fixed together with 6 in. steel nails

Chicken wire
10 ft. x 40 in. Fixed with ¾ in. staples to make an anti-slip surface

Green wood walkway

PERSPECTIVE VIEW OF THE GREEN WOOD WALKWAY

Handrail
Each section 4 ft. long

End lap
Centered on middle rail support post

Rail support post
5 ft. long
2 ft. 9½ in. apart
Set in line with other posts.
In ground to a depth of 12 in.
Touches the side of the walkway beam

Floor beam
4ft. 6 in. long

Pile

Pile
20 in. long
Set 12 in. into the ground.
Pairs positioned 17½ in. apart
and spaced 3 ft. 6 in. apart along the
length of the walkway

Horizontal secondary rails
9¾ in. long
Nailed between rail support posts.
Set 9¾ in. down from the handrail

Secondary post
Length cut to fit

Diagonal
The length and the angle of the
ends are cut to fit the space

Chicken wire
Folded in half along its
width to make a double-
layer strip 20 in. wide.
Fixed to path poles with
¾ in.-long galvanized
fencing staples

Selected path poles need
to be notched or cut back
in length to fit around the
upright posts

Path pole
3 ft. long

End lap
Joins the
walkway beams.
Centered on the
middle pair of piles

Step-by-step: **Making the green wood walkway**

Posts
Be careful not to destroy the tops of the piles

Joint
Cut the end laps on the thickest end of the wood

Level
Take your levels from the lowest pile

Cordless drill
The safe option when the ground is wet

Positioning
Center the end lap on the top of the pile

1 Mark out the site with the tape measure, pegs, and string. Cut six 20 in.-long piles and knock them into the ground with the sledgehammer to a depth of 12 in. Each pair of piles is 17½ in. apart. The distance between each pair along the length of the walkway is 3 ft. 6 in. Check with the level and make adjustments until the piles are level.

2 Take four 4ft. 6 in. lengths to make the floor beams. Use the saw, ax, and mallet to cut an end lap on one end of each beam. Lap the beams so that they are centered on the middle pair of piles. Drill pilot holes and nail the beams in place with the claw hammer. Work carefully to avoid splitting the wood.

Posts
Bang in the posts to a depth of 12 in.; make the tops level

Leveling
Check that the handrail is level

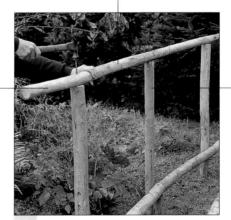

Design
The design makes possible a very slight curve if required

Handrail
Use the smoothest wood for the handrail

Upright
Use the level to ensure that the posts are upright

3 Cut three 5 ft.-long rail support posts. Set them in line and 2 ft. 9½ in. apart (so that all three posts are centered on and touching the side of the floor beam), and bang them into the ground with the sledgehammer to a depth of 12 in.

4 Prepare the handrail from two 4 ft. lengths of wood. Cut an end lap on one end of each, then nail in place so that the lapped joint is centered on the middle rail support post. Drive the nails just below the surface of the wood to ensure that the handrail is smooth to the touch.

Step-by-step: Making the green wood walkway

Nailing
Drive the nails just below
the surface of the wood

Leveling
Check the levels just prior
to fitting the diagonals

Fit
Aim for a tight
push-fit for the
secondary
posts and rails

Diagonals
The diagonals
brace the
whole structure

Pilot holes
Drill holes
when the nail
positions are
near the end of
the wood

5 Take two 9¾ in. lengths and nail them between the three rail support posts to make the horizontal secondary rails. Set the rails about 9¾ in. down from the handrail. Cut and nail the secondary posts in place. Use the level to ensure that the horizontal secondary rails and handrail are level.

6 Cut diagonals to fit, and nail them between the upright posts and below the secondary rails to make the inverted "V" pattern. Hammer the nails in at an angle, so that they are more or less at right angles to the face of the diagonals. You might need help to hold the diagonals while you drive in the nails.

Path poles
Change the path poles around until you find
an arrangement that fits together well

Chicken wire
Ease the chicken wire
to a good fit

Drilling
Drill a hole
when the nail
position is near
the end of
the wood

Double layer
You could use
two layers of
narrower wire

Stapling
Drive in extra
staples when
the wire has
settled

7 Cut 33 path poles, 3 ft. long, and nail them on top of the floor beams. Note how selected poles need to be cut back to fit around the upright posts. Arrange the poles so that their best face is uppermost, and they fit together well.

8 Fold the chicken wire in half along its width, so that it is doubled up to make a strip 20 in. wide. Fix it to the surface of the walkway with staples. The double layer of wire provides a much better non-slip surface than a single layer.

Classic stone sett patio

The pleasing thing about using stone setts is that they can be positioned with the minimum of fuss—it really is as near instant as it is possible to be. Dry-mix mortar is brushed between the imitation stone setts to complete the illusion. If you want to replicate a little bit of Victorian Britain, this is the project to choose.

TIME

A long weekend (about eight hours to prepare the site and lay the concrete, and the rest of the time for positioning the slabs, fitting the edging, and tidying up).

SAFETY

The stone setts are sharp-edged on the underside, so wear gloves and handle them with care.

YOU WILL NEED

Materials

for a patio 7 ft. x 4 ft. 3 in.

- Reconstituted stone "circle" paving setts: 100 component parts 3 1/4–3 1/2 in. wide and 2 in. thick, charcoal color (enough to make a complete circle motif at about 40 in. in diameter)
- Reconstituted stone "straight" paving setts: 200 component parts, 3 1/4–3 1/2 in. square and 2 in. thick, charcoal color (enough to add around the circle, to make a total layout that measures 6 ft. 6 in. long and 4 ft. wide)
- Rope-top edging: 12 edging components, 24 in. long, 6 in. high, and 2 in. thick, terra-cotta color (to frame and contain the paving)
- Pillar and ball posts: 4 posts, 11 in. high and 2 1/2 in. square, terra-cotta color (to link the rope edging at the corners)
- Clinker: about 8 wheelbarrow loads of builder's rubble or crushed stone waste
- Concrete: 1 part (80 lb.) cement, 2 parts (160 lb.) sharp sand, 3 parts (240 lb.) aggregate
- Mortar: 1 part (220 lb.) cement, 3 parts (660 lb.) builder's or soft sand

- Dry-mix mortar: 1 part (55 lb.) cement, 3 parts (165 lb.) builder's or soft sand

Tools

- Tape measure, long rule, and a piece of chalk
- Spade and shovel
- Level
- String line and pegs
- Formwork: wooden battens about 2 in. wide and 1 1/4 in. thick, long enough to edge all sides of the patio
- Sledgehammer
- Wheelbarrow and bucket
- Tamping beam: about 5 ft. long, 2 1/2 in. wide, and 1 1/4 in. thick
- Bricklayer's trowel
- Angle grinder fitted with a stone-cutting disk
- Bolster chisel
- Club hammer
- Broom and brush

A MAGIC SETT PIECE

The wonderful thing about stone setts is the ease with which they can be put down. With the minimum of effort and expertise, the setts can be swiftly arranged into a really convincing Victorian paving feature. The individual setts are simply bedded in sand and grouted so that they form a unified whole.

Ideally, the setts need to be set flat on a concrete slab and framed with rope-top edging. We have chosen to make a small patio on an existing area of chipped bark, but you could just as well use the product to disguise an existing concrete patio, or even to create a little sitting area in the middle of a lawn. We have used the setts to make a circle motif set within a rectangle; but alternatively, you could have several linked circles, or omit the circle and go for strips. We recommend that you visit a builder's yard to see the product, study our designs, and then carefully select the various setts so that they can be positioned with the minimum of cutting. You will see that the setts are basically square, rectilinear, and triangular.

CROSS-SECTION OF THE
CLASSIC CARPET STONE PATIO

Rope-top edging   Pillar and ball post

Carpet stone
2 in. thick

Sand
3/4 in. thick

Concrete
Approximately 2 in. thick

Clinker
3 3/4 in. thick

Classic stone sett patio

PLAN VIEW OF THE CLASSIC STONE SETT PATIO

Rope-top edging
24 in. x
6 in. x 2 in.

*Reconstituted
stone paving setts*
3¼ –3½ in.
square and
2 in thick

Gap
Lay the stone
components so
that there are
equal gaps to
all sides

*Setts in various
sizes and shapes
selected to make
a circle 40 in. in
diameter*

Edging piece
Cut to fit

Pillar and ball post
1 1 in. x 2¼ in.

EXPLODED VIEW OF THE CLASSIC STONE SETT PATIO

Surrounding area
Around the outer edges of the patio, you could plant flowers, lay turf,, or spread a ground covering such as chipped bark or gravel

Dry-mix mortar
Fill the gaps with a mixture of sand and cement powder

Mortar
A stiff mix for bedding in the edging and posts

Clinker
3¹/4 in. thick

Concrete
Approximately 2 in. thick

Rope-top edging
24 in. x 6 in. x 2 in.

Sand
³/4 in. thick (on top of concrete)

Step-by-step: **Making the classic stone sett patio**

Clinker
Make sure the clinker is free from unstable cavities

Tamping
Tamp in both directions, working right into the corners

Gloves
Wear gloves to protect your hands from the concrete

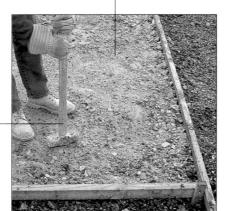

Sledgehammer
Let the weight of the hammer do the work

Concrete
Tamp several times to let trapped air escape

1 Use a spade and level to level an area measuring 8 ft. 4 in. x 5 ft. Spread an 3¼ in.-thick layer of clinker over it and peg out the formwork to make a frame 6 ft. 8 in. long and 4 ft. wide. Compact the clinker with the sledgehammer. Pay particular attention to the corner areas and edges.

2 Mix the concrete and pour it into the frame. Use the beam to tamp the concrete level with the top of the wood. Leave to set overnight. If rain threatens, cover it with plastic sheet; if there is likely to be a frost, cover it with sacking or layers of newspaper.

Carefully select
Choose the setts so that they fit the arrangement for best effect

3 When the concrete has set, remove the formwork. Spread a ¾ in. layer of sand over the concrete and carefully arrange the setts into position.

Helpful hint

When you are putting the stone setts in position, spend time carefully arranging them for best overall fit. If you have to cut the setts, then use the angle grinder, bolster chisel, and club hammer— in much the same way as when cutting the rope-top edging.

Edging
Use a level to make
checks on the edging

Hammer blows
Make little taps rather
than big ones

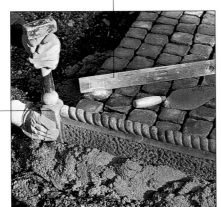

Corners
Ensure that the
corner posts
are upright

Wood block
Place under the
stone to give
an even surface
to work on

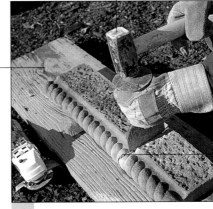

Angle grinder
Make the
scored line over
the rope detail
extra-deep

4 Starting at one corner of the patio, position the pillar and ball posts and the rope-top edging. Set them in a stiff mix of mortar (the bottom of the rope detail running along the top of the edging should be slightly higher than the surface of the stone setts). Clean off any stray mortar that has dropped on the edging and setts.

5 To cut a piece of rope-top edging, place it on a wooden board. Draw a chalk line to establish the line of cut and score it with the angle grinder. Set the bolster chisel in the groove and tap with the club hammer until the edging breaks.

6 Finally, make a pile of dry-mix mortar and use the broom and brush to spread it over the stone setts, filling all the joints. Continue until all the joints are full. This procedure must be carried out on a dry day.

Surface
You must wait
until the
surface is dry
before filling
the gaps

Brush
Use a soft-
bristled brush
to tease the
mortar into the
joints

Art Deco steps

The exciting thing about the Art Deco steps is that they lead your eye from one level

of the garden to another, and beckon you to take the route that they offer. These

attractive steps are just asking to be embellished with plants to add to their charm.

YOU WILL NEED

Materials *for 8 steps spanning 9 ft. and rising 2 ft.*

• Outer segment paving stones: 8 radius slabs, 18 in. long, 14 in. wide at the narrow end, 21 1/2 in. wide at the broad end, and about 2 in. thick (purchase slabs designed to be used as the outer ring of a circular paving kit for a patio about 8 ft. 8 in. in diameter)

• Split stone (sandstone or limestone): about 5 wheelbarrow loads

• Broken brick and/or stone waste: about 2 wheelbarrow loads

• Clinker for the foundation (either stone waste or builder's rubble): 4 wheelbarrow loads

• Cobbles and stones for decoration: quantity to suit

• Concrete:
  1 part (55 lb.) cement,
  2 parts (110 lb.) sharp sand,
  3 parts (165 lb.) aggregate

• Mortar:
  2 parts (110 lb.) cement,
  1 part (55 lb.) lime,
  9 parts (495 lb.) soft sand

Tools

• Tape measure, pegs, and string line

• Wooden leveling pegs: 10 pegs, 8 in. long

• Spade, shovel, wheelbarrow

• Sledgehammer

• Level

• Tamping beam: about 14 in. long, 2 1/4 in. wide, and 3/4 in. thick

• Mason's hammer

• Club hammer

• Bricklayer's trowel

• Pointing trowel

ONE STEP AT A TIME

Walk around your garden and see if there is an area that might benefit from a curved flight of about half a dozen steps— perhaps from the lawn to the patio, or from the house down to the garden. If your garden is pretty much all at the same level, like ours, you might even want to move in a ton or so of earth to create a mound especially for some steps.

Bear in mind that if each step slab is 2 in. thick and positioned up from the neighbouring step by 1 in., and if one step laps over another by about 4 in., then a flight of eight steps adds up to a total vertical rise of about 2 ft., and a horizontal distance of just over 9 ft. Study your garden in terms of the flow of human traffic, to decide where the steps might best be placed. When you have made sure that the area is free from drain covers and suchlike, you can get down to work.

SIDE VIEW OF THE ART DECO STEPS

4 in. overlap

1 in. up from the step below

Outer segment paving stones
2 in. thick

Split stone
Sandstone or limestone

Concrete
4 in. thick

Clinker
4 1/2 in. thick

Leveling pegs

Art Deco steps

PERSPECTIVE VIEW OF THE ART DECO STEPS

Radius paving slab
Outer segment paving stone
18 in. long x 14 in. wide at the
narrow end and 21 1/2 in. wide at the
broad end, 2 in. thick

The steps are arranged
in a suitable curve.
Each slab overlaps the other
by a minimum of 4 in.

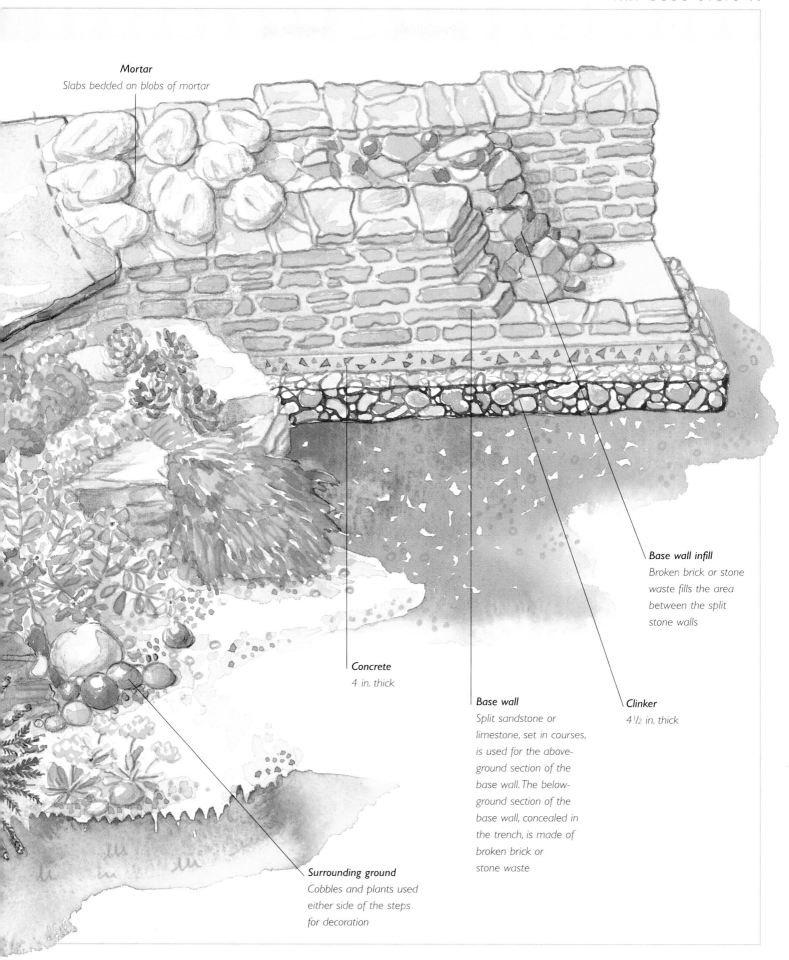

Mortar
Slabs bedded on blobs of mortar

Base wall infill
*Broken brick or stone
waste fills the area
between the split
stone walls*

Concrete
4 in. thick

Base wall
*Split sandstone or
limestone, set in courses,
is used for the above-
ground section of the
base wall. The below-
ground section of the
base wall, concealed in
the trench, is made of
broken brick or
stone waste*

Clinker
4 1/2 in. thick

Surrounding ground
*Cobbles and plants used
either side of the steps
for decoration*

Step-by-step: **Making the Art Deco steps**

Tamping
To work best, the beam needs to match the width of the trench

Leveling peg
The concrete comes up to the top of the peg

Concrete
If the weather is very wet, cut back on the amount of water in the mix

1 Mark out the position of the steps with pegs and string. Clear the earth so it is level with the bottom step, and dig out a trench to match the area of the whole flight of steps, making it 14 in. wide and 12 in. deep. Spread a 4¹/₂ in. layer of clinker, and compact and level it with the sledgehammer. Check that it is level by using the level. Hammer in leveling pegs along the trench, extending 4 in. above the clinker, about 3¹/₂ in. apart. Check that they are level with the level. Pour in a 4 in. layer of concrete, tamping it level with the beam. Leave to set overnight.

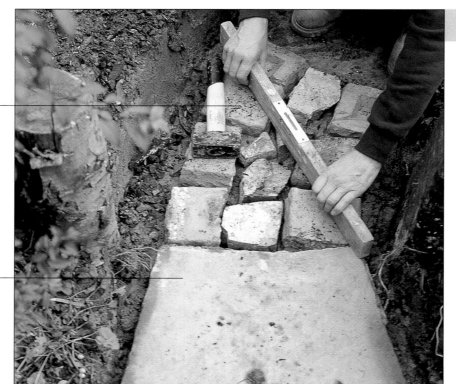

Rubble
Use any type of rubble as long as you finish up with a level surface

Base wall
The base wall is hidden below ground in the trench at this stage

2 Using the bricklayer's trowel, bed the radius slab for the bottom step on dabs of mortar. For the next step, lay a layer of broken brick and/or stone waste in the trench (to match the size of the slab), making a base wall that finishes up about ³/₄ in. higher than the first step slab. Throughout, the mason's and club hammers are used for breaking stone and tapping it into position. Spread a generous layer of mortar over the base wall, and then very carefully position and bed the second step slab so that it laps over the first.

Infill
The middle of the wall is made
from stone waste or broken brick

3 As soon as the base wall rises above the level of the trench, it is on show and so is constructed with outer walls of split stone, mortared together, and a central infill of broken brick and stone waste.

Best face
Use the best
stone for the
face of the wall
that is on view

Base wall
To ensure
that the
above-ground
part of the
wall looks its
best, build
with care for
decorative effect

4 With mortar and pointing trowel, use the split stone to build up the base wall so that it is ¾ in. higher than the second step, and then bed the third step in place as already described. Repeat the process for the remainder of the steps.

Pointing
Undercut the
pointing under
the front edge
of the steps

Helpful hint

When you are putting the slabs in position, be careful that you don't knock the walls askew—you may need help. If the weather is hot and dry, dampen the underside of the slabs prior to bedding them on the mortar.

Inspirations: Steps

The beauty of a flight of steps is that you can use it to make a design statement above and beyond its practical purpose as a means of climbing from one level to another. The wealth of materials available means that you can create something of rustic simplicity or elegant formality, or have fun with pattern and color. Steps can create a swirl of movement that links different areas into an interconnected whole.

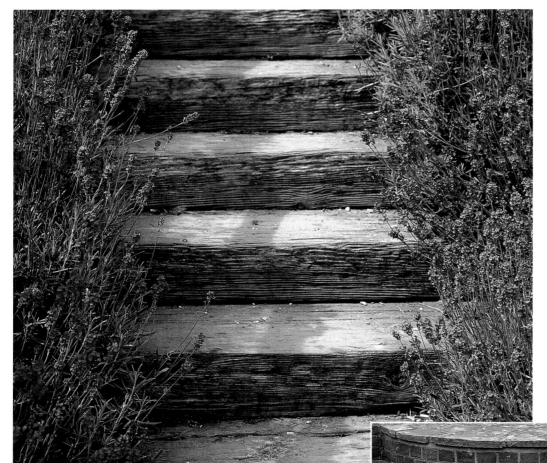

ABOVE A flight of railroad tie steps lined by banks of lavender. The flowers will release their fragrance as people brush past. A simple, effective design.

RIGHT A semicircular flight of steps to a doorway, with brick risers and "crazy"-paved treads. Note how the top riser is built using half-bricks.

ABOVE **Wide, moss-covered steps grandly lead the way up to an old country house. Their time-worn, velvety appearance establishes this as a place with a** history. Although they look beautiful, the steps have one drawback—in damp weather they are liable to become very slippery and hazardous.

Elizabethan half-circle doorstep

A doorstep is a functional way of moving from one level to another (in this case from the garden into the house), but it can also be an attractive feature in its own right. The ornate decoration of this particular step is reminiscent of knot gardens and pretty posies—perfect for those who are romantics at heart.

CROSS-SECTION OF THE ELIZABETHAN HALF-CIRCLE DOORSTEP

Inner tile segment paver
To fit around central stone

Central paving stone
One half-circle slab, 18 in. in diameter

Riser wall

Mortar

Concrete

Existing concrete path

Brick
Smooth-textured brick cut in half

YOU WILL NEED

Materials *for a doorstep about 4 ft. in diameter and 9 in. high*
• Central paving stone:
  1 half-circle slab, 18 in.
  in diameter, 1½ in. thick
• Inner tile segments:
  2 segments, internal diameter
  to fit around central paving
  stone (with ½–¾ in. gap
  allowed), external diameter
  about 36 in., 1½ in. thick
• Bricks: 25 smooth-textured
  red bricks
• Mortar:
  2 parts (24 lb.) cement,
  1 part (12 lb.) lime,
  9 parts (108 lb.) soft sand

• Concrete:
  1 part (35 lb.) cement,
  2 parts (70 lb.) sharp sand,
  3 parts (105 lb.) aggregate

Tools
• Tape measure and a piece
  of chalk
• Bolster chisel
• Club hammer
• Wheelbarrow
• Bucket
• Bricklayer's trowel
• Level
• Pointing trowel
• Shovel
• Soft-bristled hand brush

MAKING A GRAND ENTRANCE

This project draws its inspiration from Victorian steps, which themselves were influenced by steps that were made in England during the Elizabethan period. The steps are characterized by the use of a mixture of red brick and low-fired brick tiles set on edge. We have modified the design by using two inner "tile-on-edge pavers," plus a central stone paver (items really intended to be used as part of a radius paving patio kit).

The step is constructed in four stages—cutting and laying the bricks, backfilling with concrete behind the riser wall, setting the pavers in place, and pointing the joints. We were able to build the step straight off an existing concrete path, but you might have to start by laying a concrete base slab.

Cutting the bricks in half is much easier than it looks—one good blow with the club hammer and the bolster chisel usually does the job. Just be confident and brave! However, if you would prefer not to cut bricks, or simply want to slash costs, use either salvaged half-bricks or bricks that have been broken in transit. Most suppliers are able to provide broken bricks. Failing that, you could build the riser wall from whole bricks standing on end.

Step-by-step: **Making the Elizabethan half-circle doorstep**

Central paving stone
Align the half-circle with the center of the doorway

Brick
Use the brick's width to draw out the border

1 Carefully center the half-circle central paving stone and the two inner tile segments outside the door. Use a brick and chalk to draw the border around the tiles to the correct width.

Helpful hint

If possible, use hand-made red clay bricks rather than machine-made bricks, which tend to be very dense and so do not break as easily. This project requires a lot of half-bricks, so it is important that you can break them with ease. Avoid extruded bricks with holes through them and concrete bricks.

Layout
Arrange the bricks so that the gaps are wedge-shaped in top view

Best face
Position the half-bricks so that the best end is on view

Waste mortar
Scrape all the waste mortar into the half-circle

Tapping
Tap the bricks into position using the handle of the trowel

Dampening
Moisten the bricks prior to laying in place

2 Use the bolster chisel and the club hammer to break the bricks in half, until you have about 40 half-bricks. Set out the bricks (dry) so that they are standing on edge with the best end faces looking to the front and the broken ends hidden from view on the inside.

3 Remove the pavers and wet the half-bricks. Mix a stiff mortar with the bricklayer's trowel and lay the bricks to form the riser wall—one line upon another with the vertical joints staggered, and with the ends set true to the center of the circle. Check with the level.

Surface joint
The joint must be wedge-shaped
in top view

4 Use the pointing trowel to first rake out the joints to a depth of about ¾ in., and then to top them up with fresh mortar. Point the mortar so that the vertical joints are "peaked" at the center.

Pointing trowel
Use the edge of the trowel to smooth the face of the mortar

Face joint
The peak must divide the width of the joint equally

Tamping
Use the weight of the hammer to level the tiles

Pointing trowel
Use the point of the trowel to sculpt the mortar

Mortar
Butter fresh mortar over the concrete

Pointing
The mortar emphasizes the shape of the inner tile segments

Mortar
Wait 48 hours for the mortar to cure before using the step

5 Fill the recess behind the riser wall with concrete, to within 2 in. of the top. When the concrete has begun to set, butter it with fresh mortar and bed the half-circle and the inner tile segments in place. Check with the level.

6 Mix a small amount of fresh mortar and use the pointing trowel to tidy up all the joints seen on the top face. Finally, use the soft brush to remove mortar from the faces of the pavers and bricks, working with a flicking action.

Decorative Victorian path

This project takes its inspiration from a traditional Victorian townhouse with a small front garden. If you enjoy color and geometric patterns, and are planning a straight path from the gate to the front door, this classic formal path will create a striking feature. The durable materials are good for a front path, which will get a lot of use.

TIME

Three days (two days for making the foundation and one day for setting the slabs, edging, and tidying up).

SAFETY

Cement can cause skin irritation and burns—always wear gloves for mixing. Use a barrier cream as well if your skin is sensitive.

YOU WILL NEED

Materials *for a path 16 ft. 6 in. long and 38 in. wide.*
- Paving slabs or tiles—either reconstituted stone or clay terra cotta: 36 tiles, 300 x 12 in. square and 1½ in. thick (18 slate gray and 18 brick red)
- Border setts: concrete Victorian paving stone setts: 22 sections, 18 in. long, 6¼ in. wide, and 1½ in. thick (side of the path)
- Edging tiles: 30 concrete or glazed ceramic Victorian tiles, 9 in. high, 7½ in. wide, and 1¼ in. thick (to edge one side of the path)
- Clinker (builder's rubble or waste stone): about 10 wheelbarrow loads
- Pea grit: about 2 wheelbarrow loads
- Mortar: 1 part (55 lb.) cement, 2 parts (110 lb.) soft sand
- Concrete: 1 part (155 lb.) cement, 2 parts (310 lb.) sharp sand, 3 parts (465 lb.) aggregate

Tools
- Tape measure, long rule, and a piece of chalk
- String line and pegs
- Wheelbarrow and bucket
- Spade and shovel
- Sledgehammer
- Wooden battens: several, long enough to edge both sides of the path, about 2½ in. wide and 1¼ in. thick (formwork)
- Tamping beam: about 40 in. long, 2½ in. wide, and 1¼ in. thick
- Bricklayer's trowel
- Mortar float
- Level
- Piece of railroad tie or something similar, measuring approximately 16 in. long
- Angle grinder with a stone-cutting disk
- Bolster chisel
- Club hammer
- Broom

UP THE GARDEN PATH

Our path is 16 ft. 6 in. long, but the measurements of your garden will probably dictate a different length. Work out how long your path needs to be, divide our quantities by five to give you the amounts for a yard run, and then change the amounts to suit your requirements. Use the tape measure and string line to set out the path on the ground, and then stand back and see how it looks in relation to the site. There are various things to take into consideration before you start the procedure of digging out the earth to a depth of 6 in., spreading a 2½ in. layer of compacted clinker in the hole, then topping it off with a 2½ in. layer of concrete. Where are you going to put all the earth? Where are you going to put the clinker, sand, and cement when they are delivered? How are you going to get to and from the house while you are waiting for the cement to cure? You need to decide well in advance. Finally, you need to think about costs and quality. For example, we have kept costs down by using concrete slabs, but you might prefer to use top-quality materials such as stone or ceramic.

CROSS-SECTION OF THE DECORATIVE VICTORIAN PATH

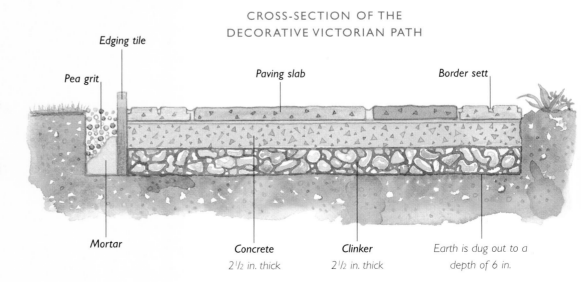

Edging tile

Pea grit

Paving slab

Border sett

Mortar

Concrete
2½ in. thick

Clinker
2½ in. thick

Earth is dug out to a depth of 6 in.

Decorative Victorian path

PLAN VIEW OF THE DECORATIVE VICTORIAN PATH

Trench
6 in. x 1 1/2 in.

Mortar
To bed edging tiles

Lawn edge

Clinker
2 1/2 in. thick

Concrete
2 1/2 in. thick

Mortar
*To bed
paving slabs*

Edging tile
9 in. x 7$^1/_2$ in. x 1$^1/_4$ in.

Border sett
1 section
18 in. x 6$^1/_4$ in. x 1$^1/_2$ in.

Pea grit

Paving slab
or tile
12 in. x 12 in.
x 1$^1/_2$ in.

Flower
border

Step-by-step: **Making the decorative Victorian path**

Concrete
Avoid damaging the fragile edge of the concrete

Bedding the setts
Use the handle of the trowel to tap the border setts into position

Formwork
When the concrete has set, remove the formwork by tapping it away from the concrete

Border setts
Bed the setts on to a generous layer of mortar

Concrete
Scrape up any blobs of mortar that drop on the concrete

1 Using string and pegs, set out the dimensions of the path (16 ft. 6 in. long and 38 in. wide). Remove the earth to a depth of 6 in., then lay a 2½ in. layer of clinker and compact it with the sledgehammer. Build the formwork. Fill with a 2½ in. layer of concrete, and tamp level with the top of the formwork.

2 Arrange all the slabs and border setts (dry) on the concrete, just to check that your calculations are correct. Next, mix a wheelbarrow load of mortar and cement the border setts in place, positioning them so that they are flush with the edge of the concrete. Check that they are level by using the level.

Club hammer
Give the chisel repeated taps with the club hammer

Tiles
Wet the tiles prior to bedding them in the mortar

Bolster chisel
Set the bolster chisel in the scored groove

Mortar
The mortar needs to be a loose, wet mix

Bedding
Ease the tile from side to side in order to bed it in the mortar

3 Trim slabs as required. With the slab positioned on the railroad tie, draw a chalk guideline from corner to corner. Score the line with the angle grinder. Set the edge of the bolster chisel in the scored groove, then tap with the club hammer until the slab breaks in half.

4 Use the trowel to spread a layer of mortar over the concrete. One at a time, dip the slabs in water, shake off the excess, and then very carefully bed them in place on the mortar. Check that they are level by using the level.

Club hammer
Tap the edging tiles into the mortar
with the handle of the club hammer

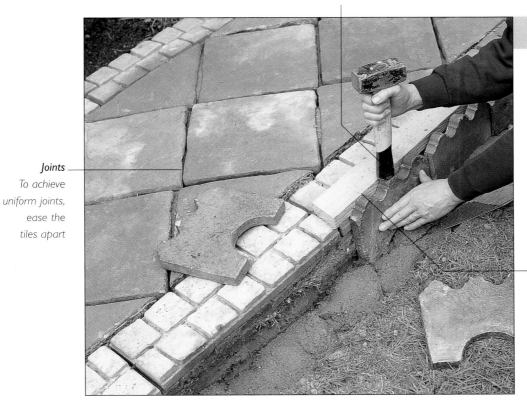

Joints
*To achieve
uniform joints,
ease the
tiles apart*

5 When the mortar has set, use the spade and trowel to dig a trench 2½ in. wide and 6 in. deep alongside the edge of the path. Shovel a generous amount of mortar into the trench, then position the edging tiles and tap them level with the handle of the club hammer. When the mortar has set, top the edging trench with pea grit.

Edging tiles
*Align the top
of the tiles
with the top of
a 1¼ in.-thick
batten placed
on the
border setts*

Dry-mix mortar
*Brush the dry
mortar into all
the joints*

6 Make a dry-mix mortar consisting of 1 bucketful of cement powder to 3 parts sand, and sweep it carefully backward and forward over the path until all the joints are filled. Finally, spray a fine mist of water over the path and leave for 24 hours before walking on it.

Helpful hint

Before you start mixing and brushing the dry-mix mortar, check that the path is absolutely bone dry. If the slabs are damp, or if it looks likely to rain before you complete the task, wait for a dry day.

Railroad tie steps

Steps made out of railroad ties are a good, practical idea, because the chunks of wood make really safe and comfortable steps. The combination of wood and stone in this design harmonize together beautifully, but the best thing about the whole structure is that it can be built without concrete. If you have a place where you need a flight of three or four steps, this the project for you.

TIME
A day (four hours for preparing the site, and the rest of the time for placing the wood and the stone).

SPECIAL TIP
Start by obtaining the sleepers, and then modify the width of the steps to fit— perhaps each sleeper can be halved to make two steps.

CROSS-SECTION OF THE RAILROAD TIE STEPS

Line indicates the level of the split stone coping edge on either side

Railroad tie
25¹⁄₂ in. x 10 in. x 6 in.

Cobbles

Ballast
3 in. thick

Step support
12–16 in. long and 3 in. in diameter, with pointed end

YOU WILL NEED

Materials *for a flight of 4 steps rising 2 ft, 25¹⁄₂ in. wide, and just under 8 ft. long*
- Railroad tie: 4 pieces, 25¹⁄₂ in. long, 10 in. wide, and 6 in. thick (steps)
- Poles: 8 split, pointed pine poles, about 12–16 in. long and 3 in. in diameter (step supports)
- Ballast: 4 bucketfuls per step
- Cobbles: 1 bucketful per step
- Builder's or soft sand: 1 bucketful per step

- Split stone (sandstone or limestone): approximately 20 plate-size stones for each step (edging)

Tools
- Tape measure
- Spade
- Wheelbarrow and bucket
- Shovel
- Sledgehammer
- Level
- Club hammer
- Hand-size block of wood
- Mason's hammer

REACHING NEW LEVELS

These steps are built within an existing rockery. However, you could also run the steps up a steep, sloping lawn, as long as they can be cut into an existing mound where the surrounding earth provides plenty of support. It's a marvelously simple system. The first step is bedded on ballast so that it is level with the lawn, more ballast is shoveled behind the tie, the second tie is positioned and held in place with the step supports, more ballast is shoveled into place, and so on. And as the steps climb up, so the space between one step and another is packed out with cobbles bedded in sand, while the bank at each side of the steps is edged with a coping of split stone. The slow rise in height from one step to another, plus the long depth to the tread, make for ease of use.

If you are making more steps than we have specified in this project, sit down with a pencil and paper and work out the most economical way to use the ties—it makes sense to get a number of whole steps out of each tie so there is no wastage. Most suppliers will cut ties to length if required.

Railroad tie steps

PERSPECTIVE VIEW OF THE RAILROAD TIE STEPS

railroad tie
25½ in. x 10 in. x 6 in.

Step support
12–16 in. long and 3 in. in
diameter, with pointed end

Edging
Split stone coping.
Plate-sized stones set on edge

Cobbles
Medium-size. Set in a
layer of sand

Ballast
6 in. thick

*Existing rockery or scree slope
(or rocks and plants can be
added afterward)*

Step-by-step: **Making the railroad tie steps**

Ballast
Use the sledgehammer to compact the ballast

1 Dig out the earth so that you have a recess about 9 in. deep, 26 in. wide, and 24 in. from front to back. Put a 3 in.-thick layer of ballast in the recess and lay the first tie so that it is level with the lawn.

Leveling
The tie needs to be level along its length but tilted slightly forward for drainage

Ballast
Some builders sell a mix of clay and crushed stone

2 Spread a 6 in. layer of ballast to the far side of the first tie and set the second tie in position. Check with the level. Use the club hammer to bang in two step supports to hold the second tie in place. Fill the area between the two ties with cobbles and a thin layer of sand.

Cobbles
Fit the cobbles so that they are packed closely together

Helpful hint

Use a watering can to dampen the cobbled area, so that the sand runs into all the nooks and crannies. Repeat this procedure after a few days to make sure the stones are tightly wedged in place.

Compacting block
*Beat the surface level
with a block of wood*

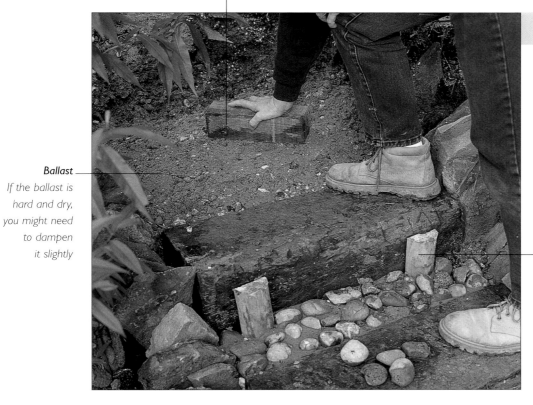

3 If you find that the ground is especially soft, or there are unexpected cavities to fill, add more ballast and spend extra time beating it firm and level with the sledgehammer. The block of wood makes a good compacting and leveling tool.

Ballast
*If the ballast is
hard and dry,
you might need
to dampen
it slightly*

Step supports
*Angle the
poles back so
that they are
pushing against
the ties*

Step supports
*Remove all traces of bark
from the split poles*

Mason's hammer
*A mason's hammer is the perfect tool
for splitting and shaping the sandstone*

Cobbles
*Positioned so
that half of
each cobble is
in the ground*

Wedge stones
*Bang small
slivers of stone
between the
coping stones*

Coping stones
*Arrange the
stones so that
there are no
sharp points
near the steps*

4 When you are banging in the step supports with the club hammer, make sure that they are pushed hard up against the leading edge of the tie, with the top of the pole banged down so that it is just below the level of the step.

5 Dig out a trench at each side of the steps and push a row of vertical coping stones into the earth to hold the whole structure in place. Tap extra stones into the cavities with the mason's hammer, to wedge the whole stack firmly.

Semicircular herb walk

A blend of plain roofing tiles, traditional red bricks, and crushed stone chippings

make this path a great decorative feature, especially when married with a miniature

herb garden. The chippings are hard-wearing and good-looking, but for cats and dogs

they are slightly uncomfortable to walk on—perfect if you want to protect your

herbs! We have used different colored chippings in each section to add interest.

YOU WILL NEED

Materials *for a herb walk 22 in. wide, 10 ft. in diameter overall, with a 5 ft. radius*
- Plain roof tiles: 50 tiles, 10¾ in. long and 6¼ in. wide—this number allows for wastage (path edgings)
- 7 reconstituted stone coping stones, 18 in. long, 7¼ in. wide, and 1¾ in. thick (edging for back of semicircle)
- Bricks: 4 bricks, 8 in. long, 3⅜ in. wide, and 2¼ in. thick (path divisions)
- Crushed stone chippings: 3 bags in color(s) of your choice—about 110 lb. each

- Plastic sheet: 20 ft. long and 40 in. wide
- Mortar:
  2 parts (70 lb.) cement,
  1 part (35 lb.) lime,
  9 parts (315 lb.) builder's or soft sand

Tools
- Tape measure, wooden pegs, and string
- Club hammer
- Spade and shovel
- Wheelbarrow
- Bucket
- Bricklayer's trowel
- Pointing trowel

A VERY TASTY GARDEN PATH

This project is a very simple affair, really no more than a semi-circular path edged with roofing tiles and sub-divided with bricks, with the resultant recesses filled with crushed stone. We used two wooden pegs joined with string to draw out a half-circle. This device was also used to scribe around the circumference to divide the path into three equal sections. We chose to build a semicircle because we wanted to butt it on to the side of an existing path, but you can build a complete circle by doubling up the materials.

The path enables you to nip out from the kitchen and gather herbs to add to your cooking without getting your feet wet or muddy in the garden. The width and depth of the path are also an advantage if you are planting herbs with invasive root systems, such as mint, because the path provides a barrier between the plants and the garden. An ideal feature for a small town garden.

CROSS-SECTION OF THE SEMICIRCULAR HERB WALK

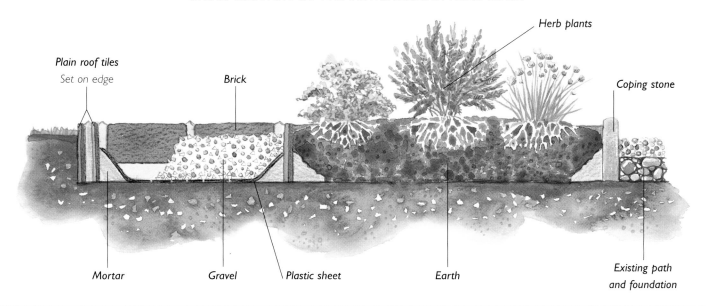

Plain roof tiles
Set on edge

Brick

Herb plants

Coping stone

Mortar

Gravel

Plastic sheet

Earth

Existing path and foundation

Semicircular herb walk

PERSPECTIVE VIEW OF THE SEMICIRCULAR HERB WALK

Large half-circle
5 ft. radius

Herb plants
*Herbs suitable for a
sunny location include
rosemary, chives, sage,
basil, and thyme*

Decorative gravel
*Crushed granite with a
sprinkling of marble*

Path division
*Bricks set level with
the tile edging*

Decorative gravel
Crushed white marble

Small half-circle
about 38 in. radius

Plastic sheet
*Spread over the earth to prevent weed growth.
Could use salvaged plastic sacks*

Roof tile edging
Set in a generous bed of mortar

Plain roof tile
10³⁄₄ in x 6¹⁄₄ in

York stone coping stone
*18 in. x 7¹⁄₄ in. x
1³⁄₄ in.*

Roof tile edging
*A tile sandwich with
a mortar filling*

Roof tiles
*Set on edge in a
staggered sequence
so that the vertical
joints are offset*

House brick
8 in. x 3³⁄₈ in. x 2³⁄₄ in.

Step-by-step: **Making the semicircular herb walk**

Scribing
Use a 5 ft. radius to scribe the circumference of the large circle; also to divide it into three equal parts

Path
The path is about 22 in. wide

Small half-circle
Use a radius of about 38 in. to set out the small half-circle

1 Take two wooden pegs and tie them together with string so that they are 5 ft. apart. Tap one into the ground (in what will be the center of the back of the semicircle) with the club hammer. Use the string as a radius to draw out a half-circle about 10 ft. in diameter. Remove the turf to a depth of 6 in. Repeat the procedure to draw a half-circle with a radius of about 38 in.

Outer ring
Set the outer ring of tiles with the best face facing outward

2 Set a single line of roof tiles in mortar around the two circumferences, using the bricklayer's trowel for moving the mortar and the pointing trowel for fine detailing.

Helpful hint

We have used relatively expensive plain roof tiles for the edging, but you could cut costs by using salvaged tiles and slates— or even a totally different material such as broken brick, wine bottles set upside down, found rocks, or broken paving slabs.

Tamping
Tap the tiles level with the
handle of the club hammer

Mortar
Use spare mortar to buttress the
tiles on the path side

Tile sandwich
The cavity
between the
tiles is filled
with mortar

Brick
Set the bricks
on edge so
that the best
face is
uppermost

Pointing
Use the point
of the small
trowel to tidy
up the mortar
in the tile
sandwich

3 Butter mortar on the inside face of
the outer edging of tiles, and run
another line of tiles alongside the first so
that the edging is two tiles thick. The tiles
are placed so that the concave surfaces
are facing each other.

4 Position the stone slabs to make an
edging for the back of the semicircle,
and mortar in place. Make the path
divisions by setting the bricks on a
generous bank of mortar, so that they are
aligned with the center of the circle.

5 Spread the plastic sheet
over the three recessed
areas. Cover the plastic with
chippings, bringing the level of the
path up to within ¾ in. of the top
of the tile edging. Plant up the
central area with herbs.

Herbs
Fill the central
area with soil
and plant with
your favorite
culinary herbs

Gravel
Spread an even
layer of gravel
over the plastic

"Crazy"-paved circular patio

A large, formal circular stone patio is a practical and pleasing garden feature. Small children love to use it for playing games; it offers a good surface for bench seats and picnic tables; it is great for displaying containers of plants; and the strong circular motif provides a counterbalance to informal areas of planting.

YOU WILL NEED

Materials *for a patio about 10 ft. in diameter*
- Antique radius brick edging: 16 x 24 in. units (designed to go round the outer edge of a paved circle about 9 ft. in diameter)
- Border radius setts (concrete Victorian-style paving stone setts): 20 sections about 20 in. long, 6¼ in. wide, and 1½ in. thick (designed to go round the inner edge of a paved circle about 9 ft. in diameter)
- Sandstone (split stone in random-size pieces): about 6 sq. yd. (this amount allows for wastage and choice)
- Formwork: 1 sheet of the thinnest and cheapest grade of plywood, 8 ft. x 4 ft., cut across the grain to make strips about 8 in. wide
- Clinker (builder's rubble or waste stone): about 6 wheelbarrow loads
- Sharp sand: about 1100 lb.
- Concrete:
  1 part (220 lb.) cement,
  2 parts (440 lb.) sharp sand,
  3 parts (660 lb.) aggregate
- Mortar:
  1 part (70 lb.) cement,
  2 parts (140 lb.) builder's or soft sand

Tools
- Tape measure, wooden pegs, and string
- Spade
- Fork
- Wheelbarrow
- Shovel
- Rake
- Saw
- Club hammer
- Bricklayer's trowel
- Length of board to use as a treading board, to spread your weight
- Level
- Length of railroad tie to use as a worksurface
- Mason's hammer

GOING ROUND IN CIRCLES

The ground in our garden is both wet and sloping, so we decided that once the clinker and sand for the foundation of the patio was in place, we would start by setting the antique brick edging on a solid concrete base. This meant that the built-up edging would not only contain and stabilize the stone paving, but once the concrete had set, it would also give us a level to work to.

It is best to start by roughly laying out the stones dry, to check that their positions are as you want them, placing the largest pieces more or less at the center of the circle. Work outward from the center, to minimize treading on the stones that are in place. The stones are then bedded in a thick mix of concrete, rather than mortar. All you do is shovel a heap of concrete on the sand, then bed and level the dampened stones in the concrete.

CROSS-SECTION OF THE CRAZY-PAVED CIRCULAR PATIO

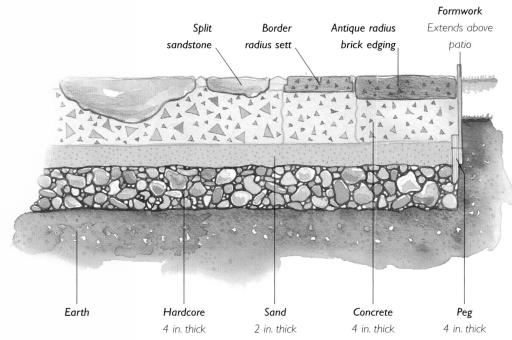

Split sandstone — *Border radius sett* — *Antique radius brick edging* — *Formwork* *Extends above patio*

Earth — *Hardcore* *4 in. thick* — *Sand* *2 in. thick* — *Concrete* *4 in. thick* — *Peg* *4 in. thick*

"Crazy"-paved circular patio

PLAN VIEW OF THE "CRAZY"-PAVED CIRCULAR PATIO

Antique radius brick edging
Designed to go around a circle about 9 ft. in diameter. Made from cast concrete

Border radius sett
Designed to go within a circle about 9 ft. in diameter. Made from cast concrete

Joints
Minimum of $1/2$ in. wide. Pointed with mortar in such a way that they form peaks or ridges at the center

Circle about 10 ft. in diameter

Split sandstone
*"Crazy" paving bedded on a
stiff mix of concrete*

Formwork
*Made from 8 in.-wide
strips of thin, flexible
plywood*

Earth
*Dug out to a
depth of 1¼ in.*

Concrete
4 in. thick

Sand
2 in. thick

Clinker
4 in. thick

Step-by-step: Making the "crazy"-paved circular patio

Formwork
Peg the strips of plywood in place to make the formwork circle

Antique radius brick edging
Push the edging hard up against the plywood

Circle
The finished plywood circle measures about 10 ft. in diameter and the walls are 8 in. high

Concrete
The antique radius brick edging is bedded on a 4 in.-thick layer of concrete

Trowel work
Use the trowel to tidy up the inside edge of the concrete

1 Use the tape measure, string, and pegs to mark out a circle about 10 ft. in diameter. Remove the earth to a depth of 12 in., and put down a 4 in. layer of clinker. With the saw and club hammer, use the pegs and plywood to build a formwork circle on top of the clinker. Fill with 2 in. of raked sand.

2 Spread a 4 in. layer of concrete around the edge of the circle and bed the antique radius brick edging hard up against the formwork. Use the trowel to cut the concrete back to the edging.

3 Repeat the procedure to bed the border radius setts hard up against the inside edge of the antique radius brick edging. Make sure that the joints between the two materials are staggered with each other.

Border radius setts
Bedded on concrete so that they are level with the antique radius brick edging

Helpful hint

The consistency of the concrete is all-important. It should be stiff enough for a handful to stand up under its own weight without slumping. Always dampen bricks and setts before bedding them in place.

Mason's hammer
Clip the edge of the stone to shape
using the mason's hammer

Leveling
Use a board and level to make sure
that the stones are level with the edging

Worksurface
A short length
of railroad tie
makes a
perfect
worksurface

Best fit
Spend time
trying for the
best possible fit

Joints
Aim for joints
of a uniform
width (a
minimum of
$^1/_2$ in.)

4 Start laying the sandstone crazy paving. To cut a stone to shape and size, rest it on the tie (with the edge to be cut to the far side) and give the edge a smart, flicking peck with the chisel end of the mason's hammer. Always wear goggles and gloves to perform this procedure.

5 Spread a 4 in. layer of concrete in the center of the circle and set the pieces of sandstone in place by wetting each stone, trying for best fit, and testing with the level. Use the club hammer to ease and tamp the stones into the concrete. Make sure that the best face of the stones is uppermost.

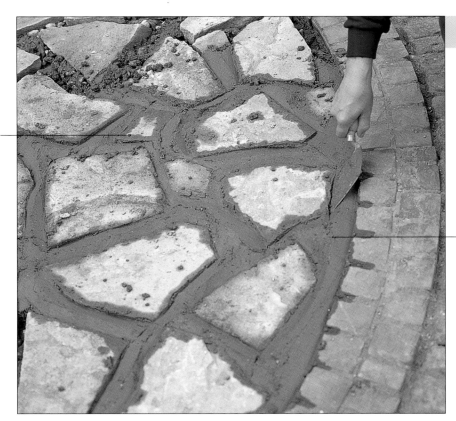

Cleaning up
Let the
mortar cure
overnight and
then clean it
up with a
stiff brush

6 Fill the gaps between the stones. Mix a heap of mortar to a smooth, buttery consistency. Overfill the joints and use the edge of the trowel to cut the pointing in toward the stone, so that the joints are ridged along the center-line.

Pointing
Sculpt the
mortar so
that the joints
are ridged at
the center

Inspirations: Patios

A patio can transform a garden. If replacing a patch of lawn or some flower beds with a patio seems like a sacrifice, remember that it will help you get more use out of the garden. A patio can become the focus for family gatherings, barbecues, or drinks parties. The choice of designs and materials is almost limitless, and a patio can even incorporate small planting pockets to break up a large expanse of stone.

LEFT This charming walled garden has a patio made from a mix of new and salvaged flagstones. The whole structure is elevated on a brick plinth, which creates the stepped or terraced effect and adds interest to a small space.

ABOVE **A** classic English patio made from salvaged bricks and granite road setts. Note that the bricks follow a grid. The design enables setts to be left out so that low-growing rockery plants can take their place.

RIGHT **A** traditional country cottage patio of flagstones and half-bricks, with some planting pockets. Thyme is especially suitable for inclusion, as it will survive being walked on and will also release its fragrance.

Snake-pattern cobble path

If you want to build a path that will withstand a lot of use and can cope with children riding on bicycles or skateboards, yet at the same time is decorative, this may be the project for you. Built on a hefty concrete slab, the snake wiggles its way through a cobbled landscape bordered by red bricks—perfect for a modern garden.

TIME

Two weekends (two days for putting down the concrete foundation and laying the bricks, and two days for bedding the setts and cobbles).

SPECIAL TIP

Try to distribute the range of cobbles (according to size and color) throughout the length of the path.

YOU WILL NEED

Materials *for a path about 10 ft. long. (This path consists of three frames. Quantities have been given for single frames, so you can increase the length of the path if desired.)*

- Border radius setts (concrete Victorian-style paving stone setts): 2 sections, about 20 in. long, 6¼ in. wide, and 1½ in. thick, for each 40 in.-long frame (designed to go round the inner edge of a paved circle about 9 ft. in diameter)
- Bricks: about 15 bricks, 8 in. long, 3⅜ in. wide, and 2¼ in. thick (for each 40 in.-long frame)
- Clinker (builder's rubble or waste stone): about 2 wheelbarrow loads for each frame
- Formwork: wooden battens long enough to edge both sides of the path, about 2½ in. wide and 1¼ in. thick
- Gravel (small-size, washed): about 2 bucketfuls for each frame
- Aggregate: about 1 wheelbarrow load for each frame

- Concrete: 1 part (55 lb.) cement, 2 parts (110 lb.) sharp sand, 3 parts (155 lb.) aggregate (approximate amounts for each frame)
- Mortar: 1 part (25 lb.) cement, 2 parts (50 lb.) builder's or soft sand (approximate amounts for each frame)

Tools
- Tape measure and chalk
- String line and pegs
- Club hammer
- Spade
- Shovel
- Wheelbarrow and bucket
- Sledgehammer
- Tamping beam: about 40 in. long, 2½ in. wide, and 1¼ in. thick
- Bricklayer's trowel
- Rake

MORE THAN JUST A PATH

This path is three frames long, but quantities have been given for single frames, so that you can easily increase the length of your chosen path. The building process is spread over a two-weekend period. The concrete foundation is put down on the first Saturday, the bricks are laid the next day when the concrete has set, and the lengthy task of positioning the setts and cobbles takes place the following weekend. As the path is presented as a series of frames—just like pictures—you could, if you so wish, complete the project frame by frame and spread it over a much longer period. It is also possible to work harder and get the project finished in a continuous three- or four-day period, but there is no escaping the fact that you do have to wait for the concrete and mortar to set. If you decide to build a path longer than three frames, it is wise to have a small expansion gap between each frame.

CROSS-SECTION OF THE SNAKE-PATTERN COBBLE PATH

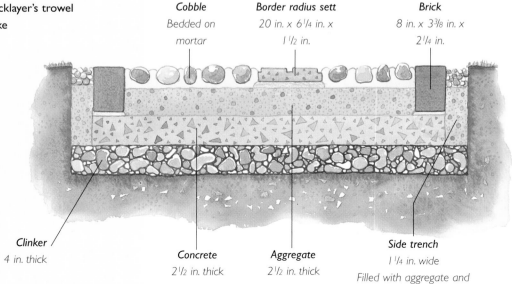

Cobble
Bedded on mortar

Border radius sett
20 in. x 6¼ in. x 1½ in.

Brick
8 in. x 3⅜ in. x 2¼ in.

Clinker
4 in. thick

Concrete
2½ in. thick

Aggregate
2½ in. thick

Side trench
1¼ in. wide
Filled with aggregate and topped with gravel

Snake-pattern cobble path

PLAN VIEW OF THE SNAKE-PATTERN COBBLE PATH

Cobbles
Bedded in mortar

Side trench
1 1/4 in. wide
When formwork is removed, the trench
is filled with 4 1/2 in. of aggregate and
topped with gravel

Brick
Set on edge in mortar with
the best face uppermost

Border radius sett
Bedded in mortar.
Two sections per frame

Aggregate
2¹/₂ in. thick

Concrete
2¹/₂ in. thick

Formwork
Wooden batten 2¹/₂ in. x 1¹/₄ in.,
set on edge. Removed prior to putting
in the aggregate and gravel infill

Earth
Dug out to a depth of 12 in.,
36 in. wide

Clinker
4 in. thick

Step-by-step: Making the snake-pattern cobble path

Path foundation
Dig out the earth to a depth of 12 in.

Tamping
Tamp the concrete level and be sure to remove air bubbles

Concrete
Fill the formwork with 2½ in. of concrete

Grass
Try not to drip concrete on the grass

Trench
Dig the trench 36 in. wide

1 Use the tape measure, string, club hammer, and pegs to set out the path, making it 36 in. wide. Dig out the earth to a depth of about 12 in. Put a 4 in. layer of clinker in the recess and hit it level with the sledgehammer.

2 Set the formwork battens on edge along the edge of the path (33 in. apart), using the club hammer to knock in pegs to hold them in position. Fill the formwork with concrete to a depth of 2½ in. and level it with the tamping beam. Keep tamping until all air bubbles have come to the surface. Leave to set.

Brickwork
Use the small trowel to point the joints between the bricks

Aggregate
2½ in. of aggregate raked over the concrete and leveled

Side trench
Fill the side trench with 4½ in. of aggregate and top with gravel

Compacting
Tamp the aggregate level with the sledgehammer

Registration marks
Draw a chalk mark on the brick to show the position of the setts

3 Remove the formwork. Use the tape measure, chalk, and one of the formwork battens to draw out the position of the bricks. Using the bricklayer's trowel, set the bricks on a bed of mortar. Fill the gap between the bricks and the lawn (side trench) with 4½ in. of aggregate and top with gravel.

4 Rake a 2½ in. layer of aggregate over the concrete and tamp it level. Position the setts (dry) on the raked aggregate and draw small chalk registration marks on the brick edging so that you know precisely where they need to be placed. Do this with all three frames.

Setts
Bed the setts on a generous spread of mortar

5 Bed the setts on mortar, so that the curve of the snake runs smoothly from one frame to another. Gently ease the setts from side to side until you are satisfied with the arrangement. Make sure that the setts are level with the bricks.

Hammer
Use the weight of the club hammer to nudge the setts into place

Leveling
Level the setts with the top face of the bricks

6 Spread and smooth a layer of mortar over the rest of the frame and bed the cobbles in place. You might need to remove some of the mortar to make way for the cobbles.

Cobbles
Ease the cobbles into the mortar until they are level with the bricks

Helpful hint

The secret of fixing cobbles firmly in place is to dampen them slightly before easing them into the mortar. Sink the cobbles until about half their bulk is hidden in the mortar. If you do not sink the cobbles far enough, they will soon come loose.

Raised decking

Raised decking is particularly appropriate for gardens that are wild and wooded, or where the ground is uneven, or those that back on to water. This type of decking can provide a vantage point and, depending on its situation, the experience can be rather like being in a treehouse, or high up on a wildlife observation platform.

TIME

Two weekends (one day for clearing the ground and sorting out your materials, one day for setting up the basic frame; the second weekend for fitting the banisters and details).

SPECIAL TIP

When you are setting up the main frame, make sure that it is both stable and square. Don't be tempted to rush.

YOU WILL NEED

Materials *for raised decking 7 ft. 4 in. square.*
(All rough-sawn pine pieces include excess length for wastage. Purchase wood that has been pressure-treated with preservative.)

- Pine: 8 rough-sawn pieces, 10 ft. long, 3 in. square section (newel posts and joist supports). Length of newel posts will vary according to the slope of your site
- Pine: 9 rough-sawn pieces, 10 ft. long, 3½ in. wide, and 1½ in. thick (joists and spacers)
- Pine: 20 pieces planed decking board, grooved or plain, 10 ft. long, 4½ in. wide, and 1¼ in. thick (floor)
- Pine: 10 rough-sawn pieces, 10 ft. long, 2 in. wide and 1¼ in. thick (banister rails and fixing battens)
- Pine: 3 rough-sawn pieces, 10 ft. long, 2½ in. wide, and 1¼ in. thick (pitch-topped rail capping)
- Pine: 14 rough-sawn pieces, 6 ft. 6 in. long, 1½ in. wide, and ¾ in. thick (temporary battens/slender balusters)
- Pine: 5 rough-sawn pieces, 10 ft. long, 6 in. wide, and ¾ in. thick (wide fretted balusters and newel post caps)

- Pine: 8 newel post finials, either turned or carved, size and shape to suit
- Zinc-plated coach bolts with washers and nuts to fit: 24 x 4½ in.
- Zinc-plated, countersunk cross-headed screws: 300 x 3½ in. no. 8, 300 x 3 in. no. 10
- Steel nails: 2¼ lb. x 5 in. x ¼ in.
- Concrete blocks: 8 blocks (post foundations)
- Clinker: 2 bucketfuls per post

Tools
- Two portable workbenches
- Pencil, rule, tape measure, marking gauge, and square
- Crosscut saw
- Cordless electric drill with a cross-point screwdriver bit
- Drill bits to fit the sizes of the nails, screws, and bolts
- Spade
- Sledgehammer
- Level
- Claw hammer
- Electric jigsaw
- Pair of clamps
- Electric sander

SIDE VIEW OF THE RAISED DECKING

Baluster assembly
Each panel is identical and fixed between the posts with screws

Finial and newel post cap
Decorative details

Joist
The joists are bolted to the newel posts

Newel post
3 in. square Supports the floor and the baluster assembly

Floor
4 in. x 1¼ in. grooved decking boards

A HIGH-RISE PATIO

The prospect of building raised decking might be a bit daunting, but it is in fact a very straightforward project. We have simplified the main frame by making it as four flat kits—two sides with two corner and one middle newel post each, and two sides with a single middle newel post each. Temporary diagonal battens hold the posts square with each other and stop them twisting during construction. Once the project is in the ground, these are knocked off and used to make the slender balusters.

The structure is a little rickety at first, but once it has been dug in and clenched with bolts, it becomes as firm as a rock. We put spacers between the floor joists. These aren't essential, but because they can be made from offcuts that would otherwise be wasted, and as they take a bit of the bounce out of the floor, we feel that their inclusion is worth the extra time and effort.

Raised decking

PLAN VIEW OF THE RAISED DECKING

Newel posts
Positioned 38 in apart

Floor
The decking boards are cut to fit through the newel posts so that they overlap the joists by ⁷/₈ in. all around

Floor
Decking boards 7 ft. 4 in. x 4 in. x 1¹/₄ in. The boards are screwed to the joists using two screws at each intersection

Spacers
Joist offcuts nailed between the joists approximately halfway along their length, but staggered as shown to allow for nailing

Joist fixing
This joist is screwed to the side of the newel post

Joist support
3¹/₂ in. x 3 in. x 3 in.

Exterior joist
7 ft. x 3¹/₂ in. x 1¹/₂ in. All the joists are the same length

Interior joist
The interior joists are distributed evenly and screwed to joist supports

PERSPECTIVE VIEW OF THE RAISED DECKING

Newel post finial
Size to suit the 3 in. x 3 in. post.
Screwed to the newel post cap

Fixing batten
32 in. x 2 in.
x 1 1/4 in.
(All the vertical
components of the
baluster assembly are
32 in. long)

Wide fretted balusters
32 in. x 6 in. x 3/4 in.
Position the decorative boards centrally
with a gap of 1/4 in. between

**Pitch-topped
rail capping**
38 in. x 2 1/2 in. x 1 1/4 in.

Newel post cap
4 in. x 4 in.
x 3/4 in.
Screwed to the top
of the post

Slender balusters
32 in. x 1 1/2 in. x 3/4 in.
Fix 3 in. away from the fixing
battens and the wide
fretted balusters

Top banister rail
38 in. x 2 in. x
1 1/4 in.

Bottom banister rail
38 in. x 2 in.
x 1 1/4 in.

Gap
The baluster assembly is
positioned 2 1/2 in. above
the level of the decking
(this makes it easier to
sweep the decking
clean)

Newel post
8 ft. 11 in. x 3 in. x 3 in.
40 in. of post extends above
the level of the joist. Posts
are 3 3/4 in apart

Newel post fixing
The posts need to be
set firmly in the ground

**Baluster
assembly fixing**
3 screws are used
both sides to fix the
assembly to the posts

Wooden stairway

Dispense with the unattractive piles of concrete blocks or old wooden boxes you've been using as steps, and ascend in style on our attractive rustic stairway. It is designed to fit the Raised Decking on page 114, but the context can be changed.

YOU WILL NEED

Materials *for a five-step stairway, 3 ft. 6 in. wide. (All rough-sawn pine pieces include excess length for wastage. Purchase wood that has been pressure-treated with preservative.)*

- Pine: 2 pieces of 3 in. square section, 10 ft. long (back newel posts)
- Pine: 2 pieces of 3 in. square section, 6 ft. 6 in. long (front newel posts)
- Pine: 4 pieces, 6 ft. 6 in. long, 4 in. wide and 1½ in. thick (stringers, stringer supports, step bearer brackets)
- Pine decking boards, grooved or plain: 5 pieces, 6 ft. 6 in. long, 5 in. wide, and 1¼ in. thick (stair treads)
- Pine: 6 pieces, 6 ft. 6 in. long, 2 in. wide, and 1¼ in. thick (banister rails and fixing battens)
- Pine: 2 pieces, 6 ft. 6 in. long, 2½ in. wide, and 1¼ in. thick (handrail capping)
- Pine: 6 pieces, 6 ft. 6 in. long, 1½ in. wide, and ¾ in. thick (slender balusters)
- Pine: 4 pieces, 6 ft. 6 in. long, 6 in. wide and

¾ in. thick (wide fretted balusters, step bearers, newel post caps)
- Pine newel post finials: 4 finials, either turned or carved, size and shape to suit
- Zinc-plated coach bolts with washers and nuts to fit: 4 x 4¾ in.
- Zinc-plated, countersunk cross-headed screws: 100 x 3½ in. no. 8, 100 x 3 in. no. 10
- Concrete blocks: 4 blocks (post foundations)
- Clinker: 1 bucketful per post

Tools
- Pencil, rule, tape measure, marking gauge, and square
- Two portable workbenches
- Crosscut saw
- Cordless electric drill with a cross-point screwdriver bit
- Drill bit to match the sizes of the screws
- Electric sander
- Spade and sledgehammer
- Level
- Electric jigsaw
- Pair of clamps

SIDE VIEW OF THE WOODEN STAIRWAY

Handrail capping
2½ in. x 1¼ in.

Wide fretted baluster
6 in. x ¾ in.

Banister rail
2 in. x 1¼ in.

Newel post finial

Slender baluster
1½ in. x ¾ in.

Newel post
3 in. x 3 in.

Stair tread
4½ in. x 1¼ in.

Stringer
4 in. x 1½ in.

A FLIGHT OF FANCY

If you are going to make these stairs to fit the Raised Decking project on page 114, keep to the sizes and amounts listed. To make alterations such as reducing the number of steps or making them narrower, you need to modify the quantities accordingly.

If you decide to have fewer steps, the angle of the stringer and banister rails stays the same, also the relationship between the

height and width of the steps; it's only the details that need to be changed. So if, for example, you want a three-tread design, all the horizontals seen in side view—the banister rails, stringers, and handrail capping—will need to be shorter. You will also need to change the design of the balusters (vertical bars).

The best way to proceed, if you simply want to build some steps up to an existing building or structure, is to start by measuring the vertical height from the ground to the doorway or structure. Once you have this measurement, you will be able to decide on the number of steps. It's not always straightforward—for instance, our site was very bumpy, and while we started out with a six-step flight, we decided in the end to bring up the level of the earth and cut down on the number of steps.

Wooden stairway

EXPLODED DETAIL OF
THE WOODEN STAIRWAY

Stair tread
37 1/2 in. x 5 in. x 1 1/4 in.
with a 1/8–3/8 in. gap between each

Stringer support
3 1/2 in. x 1 1/2 in.
Length to suit the adjoining structure
(3 1/2 ft. long if attached to the Raised
Decking on page 114)

Step bearer bracket
9 3/4 in. x 3 1/2 in. x 1 1/2 in. with
equal angled ends.
Short side measures 5 5/8 in.

Step bearer
10 in. x 6 in.
x 3/4 in.
53° angled end
The top one is fixed 8 in.
from the end of the stringer
(when measured along the
bottom edge of the stringer)

Bird's-mouth location notch
The center of this notch is
positioned 4 in. from the
end of the stringer and is
marked out using a square
and the angle of the steps
as a guide

Stair tread
Screwed to the step bearer bracket
using 2 screws at each intersection

Stringer
5 ft. 3 in. x 3 1/2 in. x 1 1/2 in.

The step bearers are positioned 3 1/2 in. apart
(when measured between their vertical sides)

PERSPECTIVE VIEW OF
THE WOODEN STAIRWAY

Newel post finial
Size to suit the 3 in. x
3 in. newel post.
Screwed to the post cap

Newel post cap
4 in. x 4 in.
x ¾ in.
Screwed to the top
of the newel post

Back newel post
10 ft. x 3 in.
x 3 in.
40 in. of post
extends above the
level of the joist

**Handrail
capping**
2½ in. x
1¼ in.
53° angled ends
Length cut to fit

Banister rail
2 in. x 1¼ in.
53° angled ends
Length cut to fit

Fixing batten
32 in. x
2 in. x 1¼ in.
53° angled ends
Three screws are
used on both
sides to fix the
assembly to
the newel posts

Fixing batten
32 in. x 2 in. x 1¼ in.
53° angled ends

Wide fretted balusters
32 in. x 6 in. x ¾ in.
53° angled ends
Shaped with the jigsaw.
Decorative balusters positioned
centrally with a gap of ¼ in.
between them

**Slender
balusters**
3¼ in. x
1½ in. x ¾ in.
53° angled ends

Front newel post
6 ft. 6 in. x 3 in.
x 3 in.
4 ft. of post
extends above
the level of the
stringer support

Bird's-mouth location notch
The same shape as the one at
the top of the steps, but the
center is positioned 2 in. from
the end of the stringer

Stringer support
Same size as the top
stringer support

The ends of the bottom
step bearers are cut to stop
at the stringer support

Step-by-step: **Making the wooden stairway**

Step bearer
Screw the step bearers to the step bearer brackets

Step bearer
Screw the step bearers, complete with brackets, to the stringer

Screw
Use three screws in the arrangement shown

Bird's-mouth location notch
Cut so the stringer fits on the stringer support

Step bearer bracket
Make sure that the step bearer brackets are square and parallel to each other

1 Take the ten step bearers and step bearer brackets (the 6 in.-wide boards and the 3½ in.-wide sections), and fix them together with 3 in. screws. You need two mirror-imaged bearers for each step. Sand them to a splinter-free finish.

2 Cut the two stringers to length. Set the step bearers on the stringers, and use 3½ in. screws to fix them in place. Saw bird's-mouth location notches at the ends of the stringers, so they will fit over the stringer supports.

Bird's-mouth location notch
The ends of the stringers are located and screwed to the stringer supports

3 Bolt the stringer supports in place on the four newel posts. Set the two stringers in position with the bird's-mouth location notches fitted on the stringer supports, and fix them with 3½ in. screws. With spade and sledgehammer, set the structure in the ground by digging a hole for each post (post length may need reducing to suit site), placing a concrete block in the bottom, lowering the frame into position, and packing clinker around the post to hold it in position. Check that the structure is true with the level.

Leveling
Make sure that the treads are level and parallel to each other

Screwing
Drill pilot holes prior to
fixing the screws

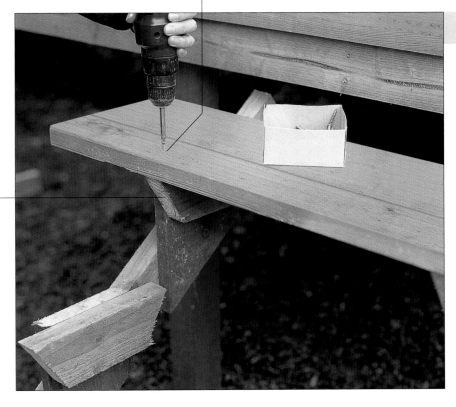

Screwing angle
Run the
screws in at
an angle to
prevent them
breaking
through the
sloped end
of the
step bearer
bracket

4 Cut the ten stair treads to length and fix them in pairs to the step bearer brackets, using 3 in. screws. Use at least two screws for each board end. Fit and fix the balusters, as shown in the raised decking project on pages 114–119 (clamped in place and screwed).

Helpful hint

When you are screwing the stair treads in place, start by fixing the bottom and top steps, so that the structure is square, then fill in with the other steps.

Newel post cap
Run a screw
through the
center of the
cap and then
screw the
cap on to the
newel post. The
central screw
is now pointing
upward

5 Cut the newel caps to size and use 3 in. screws to fit them on top of the newel posts. Study the way your chosen finial knobs need to be fixed, and center them on the newel caps. Finally, rub down the whole structure with the sander to remove splinters and sharp edges.

Newel post
finial
Drill a pilot
hole in the
end of the
finial and screw
it on to the
central newel
post cap screw

Glossary

Aligning Setting one component part against another in order to obtain best fit.

Backfilling To fill a cavity (behind a wall or in a foundation trench hole) in order to bring the ground up to the desired level.

Bedding The process of pressing a stone, slab, or brick into a bed or layer of wet mortar and ensuring that it is level.

Buttering The act of using a trowel to cover a piece of stone or brick with wet mortar, prior to setting it in position.

Butting The act of pushing one component hard up against another in order to obtain a flush fit, with both faces touching.

Centering Setting a measurement or component part on the center of another, or measuring a length or width to find the center.

Cladding Material used to cover a frame (or the process of covering a frame with wood).

Compacting Using a hammer and/or the weight of the body to press down a layer of sand, earth, or clinker.

Courses The horizontal layers of brick or stone within a wall.

Coursing The process of bedding stone and brick in mortar in order to build a course.

Curing time The time taken for mortar or concrete to become firm and stable.

Damping Wetting bricks, slabs, or stone prior to bedding them in mortar.

Dressing The act of using a hammer, chisel, or trowel to trim a stone to a level, smooth, or textured finish.

Finishing Processes such as sanding, painting, staining, pointing, or washing down, which complete a project.

Floating The procedure of using a metal, plastic, or wooden float to skim wet concrete or mortar to a smooth and level finish.

Formwork Lumber used to support the edges of concrete slabs, paths, etc. while the concrete is placed.

Leveling Using a level to decide whether or not a structure or component part is horizontally parallel to the ground, or vertically at right angles to the ground.

Marking out Variously using a pencil, rule, square, compass, pegs, and string to mark out an area.

Pointing Using a trowel, stick, or a tool of your choice to bring mortar joints to the desired finish.

Raking out Using a trowel to rake out mortar from between courses, so that edges, bricks, or stones are seen to best advantage.

Sighting To determine by eye whether or not a cut, joint or structure is level or true.

Squaring The technique of marking out, with a set square and/or level, so that one surface is at right angles to another.

Tamping The act of using a length of wood to compact and level.

Trimming Bringing wood, brick, or stone to a good finish.

Wire brushing Using a wire-bristled brush to remove dry mortar from the face of bricks, slabs or stones, for example on a wall, or the surface of a path or patio.

Index

Acknowledgments

AG&G Books would like to thank *Garden and Wildlife Matters Photographic Library* for contributing the pictures used on pages 50 (left), 51 (inset), 74, 75, 106, and 107.